# The Painful Demise of Eurocentrism

*Karl Carr* 12/26/07

# The Painful Demise of Eurocentrism:

## An Afrocentric Response to Critics

Molefi Kete Asante

**Africa World Press, Inc.**

P.O. Box 1892
Trenton, NJ 08607

P.O. Box 48
Asmara, ERITREA

# Africa World Press, Inc.

P.O. Box 1892
Trenton, NJ 08607

P.O. Box 48
Asmara, ERITREA

Copyright © 1999 Molefi Kete Asante

First Printing 1999

Library of Congress Cataloging-in-Publication Data

Asante, Molefi K., 1942-
     The painful demise of eurocentrism : an afrocentric response to
critics / by Molefi Kete Asante.
        p.   cm.
     Includes bibliographical references and index.
        ISBN 0-86543-742-4.  – ISBN 0-86543-743-2 (pbk.)
        1. Afrocentrism. 2. Eurocentrism. 3. Afrocentrism-
-Historiography. 4. Africa--Civilization--Historiography.
I. Title.
CB235.A8  1999
909'.0496--dc21                                      99-20777
                                                         CIP

# CONTENTS

# PREFACE:
## AFROCENTRIC CONCEPTS OF HISTORIOGRAPHY

To speak of the demise of Eurocentrism is not the same as to speak of the demise of Europe or of Europeans.[1] Eurocentrism in its most extreme form has generated an entire cacophony of voices that have been arrayed against the best interests of international cooperation and mutuality. It has generated a view toward the world of domination, hegemony, and control.[2] Every aspect of the gross Eurocentrism seems articulated toward this end, ultimately the subverting of international relationships. Thus, slavery, apartheid, Nazism, segregation, imperialism, intellectual arrogance, racial murders, and military and technological domination have been expressions of Eurocentrism.

It is not necessary, however, for one who is centered in a cultural space to practice the extreme versions of this ideology and therefore all people of Europe are not racists and imperialists, though it is very difficult for Europeans to escape the conditions of their historical reality. They are like passengers on a giant balloon that contains a captain who is intent on destruction. How to prevent the captain from carrying out his destruction becomes the responsibility of those who are in the balloon as well as those who would be victims; otherwise, in the end all will be victims of a rampant and rapacious racial doctrine. That is why I have always distinguished between Eurocentrism and extreme or abnormal Eurocentrism.[3] The first is a natural consequence of one's living conditions and the second is the result of an ideologically driven desire to make a particularism universal or to express a type of Western triumphalism that reduces other people to the margins of history. Such an ideology is hopefully on the demise because it is intellectually vapid, scientifically unsupportable, and ethically unsound; it is therefore not useful in the next millennium. Therefore, its demise, however painful, is expected and must be pursued in order to move forward toward a healthier world. Europe is no longer the definitional universal and the idea of race, first articulated by Europe, has come to be baggage that must be discarded. Yet we must know that it is superfluous baggage in order to discard it and move towards a world where the use of race as a descriptor is no longer valid.[4]

It is my intention to show that Eurocentrism in historiography is at the base of much of the intellectual arrogance that now confronts us in the academy and elsewhere. Scholarly journals, theatrical productions, scientific terminology, social science books, and religious texts chosen by professors are often connected and integrated into the European racial domination system that must be defeated in order to have a more just national and international society. Decent people should find the proposal for a more open world, full of mutuality, non-threatening and welcome. In presenting my ideas I am necessarily a redemptionist (Leonard Jeffries has called this thrust "Ra-demption," after the deity Ra of ancient Kemet), attempting to answer the issues raised by those who have specifically attacked the thrust for African agency that I have called Afrocentricity.[5]

By way of introducing the general idea of Afrocentricity once again, let me say that it is a fundamental necessity for African liberation at the level of psychological, economic, social, and cultural responses to the environment. For nearly five hundred years, half of a millennium, Africans were forced off of physical, cultural, political, religious, and economic terms and assigned to either the terms of the Europeans, Arabs, and Turks on the one hand and the Christians and the Muslims on the other. All African ideas were suspect, regardless of their provenance or their richness; they were not the ideas of others and consequently were pushed to the side, stolen, or subverted. I write defensively and as a redemptionist because I have, that is, as a part of the African people, been criticized unjustly, threatened in my own house, and had my own cultures relegated to the outskirts of my own intellect. Afrocentricity is the relocation, the repositioning of the African in a place of agency where instead of being spectator to others, African voices are heard in the full meaning of history. Why this should be a threat to others will become clearer in the analysis I shall make of some of the principal critics.

Now the demise of Eurocentrism is necessary because it structures a set of values and insists on a framework that views Africa and Africans in a junior light. This is a formula for constant intellectual revolt and physical violence; one must choose either to engage in a legitimate quest for mutuality or an inevitable struggle for dominance. I have always believed that Eurocentric arrogance expressed as a white supremacy view was at the heart of most mistrust and injustice in the world. This view may have been extreme at one time, because I did not have the ability to make an assessment of the totality of the ideology's reach into the core of Eurocentric education. And although there remains gaps in my understanding, I believe that I understand enough, have read enough, and reflected enough to examine the extent to which the argument against Afrocentricity has been founded on a white supremacist Eurocentrism; even *black* critics are using white supremacy to attack Afrocentricity. One does not have to be white to be an advocate of white supremacy, as has been shown in the works of Kwame Appiah, Gerald Early, and Stanley Crouch.

## CONCEPTIONS OF HISTORY

Cheikh Anta Diop, the late Senegalese scholar, was inarguably the dominant Afrocentric thinker of the twentieth century.[6] Although his works gained ready acceptance in the United States after he was introduced to the scholarly community by the lectures and papers of John Henrik Clarke, it has taken much longer for Diop to make the same impact on the African continent. Strug-

gling against the entrenched orthodoxy of the Eurocentric analyses of Africa, Diop almost singlehandedly turned the intellectual
tables on a tradition that, for the most part, had seen Africa as a
subset of the European experience. Now an entire school of
Diopian thought has emerged on both sides of the Atlantic, bringing together scholars who are committed to the demise of a
Eurocentrism in the analysis of African ideas because that analysis has soiled African scholarship with white racist thinking.

It was my own intellectual and personal encounter with Cheikh
Anta Diop in the 1980s that affirmed my theoretical and method-
ological work on the Afrocentric idea. Diop's contribution to scholarship rests essentially on his re-interpretation of perspectives of
historical facts that gave him new and more powerful answers to
the puzzles in African historiography and cultural studies. Where
European and American scholars had spoken of the multiplicity
of cutures in Africa, Diop saw unity.[7] Where they saw influences external to Africa in the Nile Valley, Diop saw the Nile as
rising in the interior of Africa and flowing down toward the Mediterranean. And where they had buried the records of ancient
Greek writers on Africa under a pile of loose interpretations, he
resurrected these writings for a new generation. Where they had
merely seen mummies, Diop saw these preserved corpses as the
source of much scientific proof that the ancient Egyptians were
black-skinned and had "wooly hair." There was in his mind no
doubt that the African continent was naturally a single cultural
entity connected by the dynamic dissemination of Nile Valley
concepts which became more diffuse as various waves of mi-
grants left the East African Rift Valley area.

Throughout Diop's life, his intellectual arguments resonated
to the tune of one over-arching thesis that Ancient Egypt is to
Africa and African peoples as Greece is to Europe and European
people and that the ancient Egyptians were black-skinned. Almost every research project or scholarly inquiry he undertook
was directed toward the support of this thesis and its corollary
that the Pharaonic Egyptians, of the same family as the Nubians,
were black.

Cheikh Anta Diop's attempt to solve another part of the puzzle of African historiography, that is, the origin and nature of African unity, led to the original publication of *The Cultural Unity of Black Africa*. Thus, as he had done originally in earlier works, Diop takes on leading European thinkers in an attempt to show the inadequacy of their arguments in relationship to the idea of matriarchy. He makes a straightforward case against the writings of J.J. Bachofen, L. M. Morgan, and F. Engels. This is the first time that he confronts the patriarchy devised by Europeans to support male dominance.

Using the concept of matriarchy as a starting point, Diop argues that African culture is united because the evidence from social history shows a divergence from the history of Europe. According to Diop, Bachofen had maintained that in its earliest stage humanity was barbaric and sexually promiscuous. Thus, descent could only be reckoned through the female since it was impossible to know the paternity of a child.

There was no marriage at this stage. During a second gynaecocratic stage, marriage was conceived, but descent remained through the female line. A third stage was called patriarchy, or masculine imperialism. Bachofen's idea was based upon Darwinian evolutionary theory. In contrast, Morgan's thesis was simply racist, according to Diop, who held that Morgan's views of marriage and kinship were not merely Eurocentric but ethnocentric as well. Using the Iroquois as an example, Morgan posited four stages of social development. He identified matriarchy with sexual promiscuity, barbarism, and the lack of civilization, whereas patriarchy and monogamy were called aspects of civilization. Engels simply used the theories of Bachofen and Morgan to argue that patriarchy subjugated women.

Diop's own research convinced him that there were two cradles of civilization, the Northern Cradle and the Southern Cradle. He compared the two systems on the basis of dowry, respect for women, kinship, disposition of corpses, and inheritance. Clearly, there were differences between the Northern Cradle and the Southern Cradle in many areas of social practice. With xii *The Painful Demise of Eurocentrism*

this structure in place, he examined the European arguments against the unity of African culture. While additional work needs to be done on this aspect of Diop's theory, it is a remarkable advance in the science of culture beyond what had been offered previously.

Indeed, where European and American scholars had argued that there were many cultures, Diop shows that the varieties of African experiences gravitate around a single matrilineal center like some massive magnet pulling the pieces together into one coherent whole. His argument unfolds on the basis of linguistic, philosophical, and cultural evidence.

A skilled researcher with an eye for detail, Diop demonstrates both pre-colonial unity and contemporary unity of African culture. This is not to say that specific variations do not exist, but rather that particular histories are nothing more than a part of the grand flow of African culture. His insight in this area has been supported in the works of Wade Nobles and C. T. Keto. Just as one speaks about Arab culture, or about European or Asian culture, one can and should speak about African culture. This demonstration is critical to the support of Diop's theses on the anteriority of Egypt to other African civilizations and to the commonality or universality of the African cultural experience in the continent.

Chris Gray's critique, called *Conception of History: Cheikh Anta Diop and Theophile Obenga,* must be viewed as the first serious and penetrating account of the work of both scholars in English.[8] Theophile Obenga is one of the leading continental scholars in the Diopian School and, much like Diop, his work has impacted upon Afrocentric scholars in the United States. Obenga is a Congolese who has served as the director-general of the Centre International des Civilisations Bantu (CICIBA) in Libreville, Gabon, taught ancient Egyptian civilization at Temple University, history at the University of Brazzaville, and African American Studies at San Francisco State University.

There are three main considerations in Gray's account of the work of Diop and Obenga. First, Gray believes that Diop and

Obenga's works have been criticized for being political because the writers have used a "macro" approach to African history. Secondly, he asserts the need to examine the social context for the production of knowledge, particularly as it is related to the debate between Africanists and Africologists, i.e., those who adopt an Afrocentric perspective on African phenomena. Thirdly, Gray provides an argument for dialogue between the Diopian school and others in the quest for a valid historiography of Africa.

The assertion that Diop and Obenga's ideas are political or have been considered political minimizes the impressive scientific work accomplished by both scholars. Gray is correct to recognize the value of "argument from evidence" and of the acceptance of the same criteria for evaluating evidence in order to advance knowledge.

Whenever scholars have examined the work of Diop and Obenga in a clear, objective fashion they have admitted, as at the Cairo Conference of UNESCO in 1974, the extensive array of data amassed to support the blackness of the ancient Egyptians by these two scholars and their followers.

But the debate over the nature of the scientific evidence is often reduced to an argument over the political nature of science itself. Of course Diop and Obenga would object, as other Afrocentrists do, to the "micro" studies that tend to view African societies or civilizations as dis-embodied, disconnected, isolated, discreet, and detached entities with no organic relationship to any other societies or civilizations. Unlike Africanists who are trapped in a single disciplinary track, Diop and Obenga base their work on evidence from many disciplines. In fact, interdisciplinarianism is one of the primary principles in the Afrocentric method. Afrocentric scholars are encouraged to examine phenomena with all of the instruments at their disposal. This might mean linguistic, anthropological, historical, ceremonial, or mythic evidences. The vast training and wide intellectual experiences of Diop and Obenga are clearly responsible for the strength of their research.

Gray points to the "dialogue with the deaf" syndrome that has greeted their work in some circles in Africa and Europe.

However, African American scholars have embraced both thinkers as critical to the re-establishment of an Afrocentric frame of mind on the continent. Prior to his death in 1986, Diop travelled to the United States on a rare visit and was feted by the African American intellectual community appearing in key social and educational settings. On the other hand, Obenga had been a student at the University of Pittsburgh where he earned a Master's degree and returned to teach at Temple University during the middle of the 1990s. Both Diop and Obenga have advanced the thinking of African scholars regarding ancient Africa at the same time as they have critiqued Eurocentric conceptions of African history. Why should African societies or civilizations be examined as sub-sets of the European experience? Why should Africans be seen as objects rather than as subjects in our own history?

Chris Gray has done exciting preliminary work on the general contours of Diop and Obenga's thought but a full discussion of their research in the light of the Afrocentric critics still needs to be done. Significantly, Gray's critique of Obenga's conception of history follows closely the guiding principles of his work on Diop. But what is different here is Obenga's own perceptive use of language to assist in the reconstruction of African history. Indeed, Obenga goes beyond Diop in his insistence on the need to articulate valid classifications in order to guide the pursuit of science. Where Diop may be said on occasion to chop down the tree with precise strokes, Obenga employs the tools of the expert sculptor to cover every imperfection.

For example, Obenga rejects "ethnohistoire" whereas Diop continued to use it into the 1980s. Obenga is content to argue the case for African scholarship on its own grounds and merits and not as an appendage to the European enterprise. His Afrocentric location is therefore more refined, perhaps more conscious than that of Diop, particularly on the question of linguistic usage. Like the Afrocentrists, Obenga recognizes the imprisonment imposed on people by the rhetorical condition itself. If one says Bushman, Hottentot, ethnohistory, ethnomusic, or minority, one is engaging in a rhetorical activity that has been defined by those outside of Africa and one is doing so to the intellectual and social disadvantage of Africa.

Unfortunately, Obenga's book on the African origin of philosophy, published in 1990 and modeled upon Diop's work on the African origin of civilization, had not appeared prior to Gray's analysis. In this volume, Obenga argues that philosophy had its beginning in ancient Egypt, not in Greece as many European writers had insisted. Furthermore, he declares that "It is difficult to understand why they are so against the simple proposition that African history should be examined and understood first by those who made it—African people."[9] He tackles the assertions of the opponents of an African agency in history by demolishing many of their ideas.

Using evidence from history, linguistics, and geography he builds a case for viewing the Nile Valley as the cradle of reason and the source of wisdom teachings. Nevertheless, Gray is able to discern the underlying patterns in Obenga's thinking about questions of usage. For example, he writes that "Obenga wants to replace Afro-Asiatic with a classification he names Negro-Egyptian, thus separating Egyptian from Berber and Semitic, and linking it with the languages of black Africa."[10] Furthermore, Gray must be credited with having pointed out the profound silence among white scholars with regard to Obenga's reworking of Greenberg's schema on African languages. Inasmauch as Obenga is an accomplished African linguist as well as Cheikh Anta Diop's intellectual heir, his work will receive increasing attention in the years to come, especially in the area of African linguistic connections.

Chukwunyere Kamalu's *Foundation of African Thought* is a synthesis of many Afrocentric researches rather than an original statement of African thought.[11] What the author seeks to do is to present the ancient foundations of African thought in such a way as to capture the essential elements and concepts of the African world. Viewing the African continent in the same way as Diop and Obenga, that is, as a cultural unity, Kamalu reconstructs the general categories of African thought from the works of many writers. The derivative nature of the work does not, however, lessen its informative value to a wider reading audience.

Many of the authors and works cited by Kamalu are hardly household names among European scholars. Although Kamalu seems to be unaware of works such as C. T. Keto's small but important volume, *The Africa Centered Perspective on History* and Linda James Myers' pioneering work, *Understanding the Afrocentric Worldview* he is clearly sympathetic to the views expressed in these works. Perhaps because Kamalu's book seems to be groping along without a clear theoretical idea, it falls short of the promise suggested in its title. Nevertheless, the author integrates Diop, Ben-Johannan, Van Sertima, Karenga, Fanon, Nketia, Amadiume, and Davidson into a brilliant synthesis of African ideas. While Kamalu is apparently unaware of the basic Afrocentric theoretical works being written on the continent and in the African Diaspora, he shows great familiarity with the seminal historical accounts of the African past as conceived by Afrocentric thinkers. The real value of this work is its integrative and pan-African perspective and in that regard it is essential for the advancement of critical thought in the field. One of the more important and significant omissions in Gray's analysis, and one that has rarely been dealt with in other critiques of Obenga and Diop, is the use of the term "Black Africa," a term which many Afrocentrists reject. In discussing this point with Theophile Obenga several years ago, he informed me that he and Diop had considered the idea of Black Africa as a matter of emphasis. They certainly believed that Africa was a black continent despite the redundancy in their terminology. To underscore the idea that the ancients were Black people they wrote "Black Africa" so there was no mistake with Arab Africa or any other type of Africa. In this way they undercut the negations of Africa that were often heard and read in the European circles about Black Africa. Cheikh Anta Diop and Theophile Obenga confronted the challenge intellectually as they had done in the 1974 UNESCO meeting of Egyptologists discussing the "Peopling of Ancient Egypt." At that conference they had presented overwhelming evidence of the authentic blackness of the Pharaonic Egyptians. Europe obviously hsa a problem with Egypt being in Africa and the ancient Egyptians being black. However, whether European writers seek to make a black Africa or a white Egypt, they are merely expressing an ahistorical response to the fact that the most complex civilization in antiquity was African black.

# AFROCENTRICITY, RACE, AND REASON

There is a long line of activist and intellectual precursors to the theory of Afrocentricity. Indeed it is in their works, organizational and theoretical, that Afrocentricity is first suggested as a critical corrective to a displaced agency among Africans caused by the physical and psychological removal of Africans by the European Slave Trade. A few of the more prominent names that recur in my own corpus of work are Alexander Crummell, Martin Delaney, Edward Wilmot Blyden, Marcus Garvey, Paul Robeson, Anna Julia Cooper, Ida B. Wells-Barnett, Larry Neal, Carter G. Woodson, Willie Abraham, Frantz Fanon, Malcolm X, and the later W. E. B. DuBois.[1] Among contemporaries the works of Maulana Karenga, Chinweizu, Ngugi wa Thiong'o, J. A. Sofola, Aboubacry Moussa Lam, Yuan Ji, Sandra Van Dyke, Terry Kershaw, Sharmarka Keita, Ayi Kwei Armah, Wade Nobles, Walter Rodney, Leachim Semaj, Marimba Ani, Na'im Akbar, Fabanwo Aduana, Abu Abarry, Charles Finch, Asa Hilliard, Kariamu Welsh Asante, Clenora Hudson-Weems, Ama Mazama, Mwalimu Shujaa, Winston Van Horne, Tony Martin, Errol Henderson, Troy Allen, Theophile Obenga, and Cheikh Anta

Diop have been most helpful and inspiring in defining the nature of the Afrocentric school of thought.[2] I hasten to add that they have all been activists, not mere armchair theorists. And quite contrary to published reports about the capability of these scholars they are all university trained in theory and methodology in several fields and many of them read and speak numerous languages, including Mdw Ntr, Greek, Latin, Zulu, and Kiswahili.

The principal motive behind all of their works seems to have been the use of knowledge for the cultural, social, political, and economic liberation of African people by first re-centering African minds, because they believed that without such liberation there could be no social or economic struggle that would make sense. None wrote simply for the sake of self-indulgence; none could afford to do so because the dispossession was so great and the myths so pervasive. Passion is never a substitute for argument as argument is not a substitution for passion, and in the intellectual arena we may disagree over finer points of interpretation; but the overall project of relocation and reorientation of African action and data has been the rational constant in all of the works of these activist scholars. I am heir to that tradition with all of its contradictions.

Although a number of writers and community activists growing out of the Black Power Movement of the 1960s had increasingly seen the need for a response to marginality, Afrocentricity did not emerge as a critical theory and a literary practice until the appearance of two small books by the Amulefi Publishing Company in Buffalo, New York. The press published Kariamu Welsh's *Textured Women, Cowrie Shells, Cowbells,and Beetlesticks* in 1978 and my book *Afrocentricity* in 1980.[3] These were the first self-conscious markings along the intellectual path of Afrocentricity, that is, where the authors, using their own activism and community organizing, consciously set out to explain a theory and a practice of liberation by re-investing African agency as the fundamental core of our sanity. Welsh's book was a literary practice growing out of her choreographic method/technique, *umfundalai*, which had been projected in her dances at the Center for Positive Thought which she directed. On the other hand, *Afrocentricity* was based on my work as leader of the Los Angeles Forum for Black Artists (the UCLA chapter of the Student Nonviolent Coordinating Committee) and as Director of the UCLA Center for Afro-American Studies in the late 1960s and early 1970s, as well as my observation and textual analyses of what people like Welsh and Maulana Karenga and Haki Mahdubuti were doing with social transformation at the cultural level. Based on the lived experiences of African people and my own peasant background from Georgia, and from what I saw in North America, the Caribbean, and Africa, the Afrocentric idea had to be concerned with nothing less than the relocation of subject-place in the African world. In my view, more adamant now than ever, this was the only approach to any other liberation for a people dislocated by circumstances of white racial supremacy. While Stephen Howe erroneously calls my thought, based on my upbringing in the South, Manichean, he is correct to see its impact on my current intellectual outlook, as I cannot divest myself of my cultural experience. But neither can Stephen Howe divest himself of his cultural outlook as his book *Afrocentrism* has clearly demonstrated. It is a book of little objectivity and much gossip as I shall show in a later chapter.[4]

A journal titled *The Afrocentric World Review* had been published in three issues in Chicago in the 1970s, but Afrocentric merely appeared as a part of the title; the articles were about the political and social issues confronting African people, and no attempt was made to lay out a theoretical basis for analysis. Thus, the two books *Textured Women* and *Afrocentricity* formed the early documents of what was to become the most discussed African intellectual idea since the Negritude Movement. They posed two important questions: How do we see ourselves and how have others seen us? What can we do to regain our own accountability and to move beyond the intellectual plantation that constrains our economic, cultural, and intellectual developmnet? These became the crucial questions that aggravated our social and political worlds.

As a cultural configuration, the Afrocentric idea was distinguished by five characteristics: (1) an intense interest in psychological location as determined by symbols, motifs, rituals, and signs; (2) a commitment to finding the subject-place of Africans in any social, political, economic, or religious phenomenon with implications for questions of sex, gender, and class. (3) a defense of African cultural elements as historically valid in the context of art, music, and literature and a defense of a pan-African cultural connection based on broad responses to conditions, environments, and situations over time; (4) a celebration of "centeredness" and agency and a commitment to lexical refinement that eliminates pejoratives, including sexual and gender pejoratives, about Africans or other people; and (5) a powerful imperative from historical sources to revise the collective text of African people as one in constant and consistent search for liberation and Maat.

Essentially, these have remained the principal features of the Afrocentric critical theory since its inception, although a number of scholars have added dimensions to the original conceptualization. I mean the works of Norm Harris, C. T. Keto, Patricia Hill Collins, Miriam Maat Ka Re Monges, Aisha Blackshire-Belay, Linda James Myers, Terry Kershaw, Wade Nobles, and Ama Mazama, among others. What all of these scholars have seen is the sheer penetrating revolutionary caliber of this idea as it relates to a re-ordering of perspectives around questions of African action, political, economic, cultural, or social action. There is a serious difference between commentary on the activities of Europeans, past and present, and the revolutionary thrust of gaining total African liberation through the re-orientation of African interest in every sphere, breaking with the fringes of Europe in an effort to be free.

Perhaps because of the rise of this idea at a time when Eurocentric scholars seemed to have lost their way in a dense forest of deconstructionist and postmodernist concepts challenging the prevailing orthodoxies of the Eurocentric paradigm, we have faced a deluge of challenges to the Afrocentric idea as a reaction to postmodernity. But it should be clear that the Afrocentrists, too, have recognized the inherent problems in structuralism and Marxism, with their emphasis on received interpretations of phenomena as different as the welfare state and e.e. cummings' poetry. Yet the issues of objectivity and subject-object duality, central pieces of the Eurocentric project in interpretation, have been shown to represent hierarchies rooted in the European construction of the political world. In fact, in the revised version of my book, *The Afrocentric Idea*, I wrote that "objectivity is a sort of collective subjectivity of Europeans."[5] This was quite in line with Marimba Ani's observation that the reification of objects is about control.

The aim of the objectivity argument, it seems, is always to protect the status quo because the status quo is never called upon to prove its objectivity, only the challengers to the status quo are asked to explain their objectivity. And in a society where white supremacy has been a major component of the social, cultural, and political culture, the African will always be in the position of challenging the white-racial-privilege status quo—unless, of course, he or she is co-opted into defending the status quo, which happens with enough regularity in this country.

In an extensive discussion of the subject-object, speaker-audience relationship, I explained how the subversion of that configuration was necessary in order to establish a playing field based on equality. But to claim that those who take the speaker or the subject position vis-a-vis others counted as audiences and objects are on the same footing is to engage in intellectual subterfuge without precedence. On the other hand, it is possible, as the Afrocentrists claim, to create community when one speaks of subject-subject, speaker-speaker, audience-audience relationships. This allows pluralism without hierarchy.

As applied to race and racism, this formulation is equally clear in its emphasis on subject-subject relationships. Of course, this subject-subject relationship is almost impossible in a racist system or in the benign acceptance of a racist construction of human relationships (as may be found in the American society and is frequently represented in the literature of several scholars who have African ancestry but who are clearly uncomfortable with that fact). White supremacy cannot be accommodated in a normal society and therefore when a writer or scholar or politician refuses to recognize—or ignores— the African's agency, he or she allows for the default position—white supremacy—to operate without challenge and thus participates in a destructive mode for human personality. If African people are not given subject place, then we remain objects without agency, intellectual beggars without a place to stand. There is nothing essentially different in this enslavement from the previous historical enslavement except our inability to recognize the bondage. Thus, you have a white-subject and black-object relationship expressed in sociology, anthropology, philosophy, political science, literature, and history rather than a subject-subject reality. It is this marginality that is rejected in the writings of Afrocentrists of the Temple Circle, which I represent as one member.

The ancient African Egyptian term *seba* first found in an inscription on the tomb of Intef I from 2052 B.C.E. had as its core meaning in the *Medu Netcher,* the "reasoning style of the people." The reasoning style of Eurocentric writers often serves the bureaucratic function of "locking" Africans in a conceptual cocoon, which seems, at first glance, harmless enough; nevertheless, the reasoning supports the prevailing positions. How can an African liberate himself or herself from these racist structures? Afrocentrists take the position that this is possible—indeed, essential—but can only happen if we search for answers  in the time-space categories which are anti-hegemonic. These are categories which place Africa at the center of analysis of all historical and contemporary African issues and African people as agents in our own contexts. Otherwise, how can we ever raise practical questions of improving our agency in the world? The Jews of the Old Testament asked, how can you sing a new song in a strange land? The Afrocentrists ask, can the African create a liberative philosophy from the icons of mental enslavement?

There are certainly political implications here because the issue of African politics throughout the world becomes one of securing a place on which to stand, unimpeded by the interventions of a decadent Europe which has lost its own moral way. This is not to say that all Europe is bad and all Africa is good. To even think or pose the issue in that manner is to miss the point I am making. Yet I know, from experience, that this will be misunderstood. So let me hasten to say that, for Africa, Europe is dangerous; it is five hundred years of danger for Africans—and I am not now talking of physical or economic danger, (though that history is severe enough), but psychological and cultural danger, the danger that kills the soul of a people. One knows, I surmise, that a people's soul is dead when it can no longer breathe its own philosophical air and when the air of another culture seems to dominate every aspect of conscious life. Following Frantz Fanon, the Afrocentrists argue that it is the the *assimiladoes*, the educated elite, whose identities and affiliations are killed first. Fortunately their death does not mean that the people are doomed; it only means that the assimiladoes can no longer be trusted to speak what the people know because they are dead to the culture, to the human project.

Afrocentricity stands as both a corrective and a critique. Whenever African people, who collectively suffer the experience of dislocation, are relocated in a centered place—that is, with agency and accountability—we have a corrective. By re-centering the African person as an agent, we deny the hegemony of European domination in thought and behavior, and then Afrocentricity becomes a critique. On the one hand, we seek to correct the sense of place of the African and on the other, we make a critique of the process and extent of the dislocation caused by the cultural, economic, and political domination of Europe. It is possible to make an exploration of this critical dimension by observing the way European writers have defined Africa and Africans in history, political science, and sociology. To allow the definition of Africans as marginals and as fringe people in the historical processes of the world is to abandon all possibility and all hope of African agency and allow Africans to become only the amaneuensis for Europe in its most degraded form.

Thus, the aims of Afrocentricity as regards the race (or, more appropriately, the cultural idea) are not hegemonic. Though I have been called by Stephen Howe "the godfather of Afrocentrism," I have no interest in one race dominating another; I am an ardent believer in the possibility of diverse populations living on the same earth without giving up their fundamental traditions except where those traditions invade other peoples' space. Then one must negotiate in good faith to share space. This is precisely why the Afrocentric idea is essential to human harmony. The Afrocentric idea represents a possibility of intellectual maturity, a way of viewing reality that opens new and more exciting doors to human understanding in spite of the European's quest to trivialize the idea as some kind of anti-white philosophy. I do not object to viewing it as a form of historical consciousness, but it is more than that: it is an attitude, a location, an orientation. To be centered is to stand some place and to come from some place; the Afrocentrist seeks for the African person the contentment of subject, active, agent place. Why this should trouble Europe and the European project is a central question of the white world's psychology.

# THE MYTH OF UNITY IN AMERICA: RE-READING ARTHUR SCHLESINGER, JR.

The nature of the frontal attacks on African Americans in the Academy on Afrocentric scholarship by academic colleagues is varied and multi-faceted. At some institutions, the dominant assaults on the African faculty come from administration policies and at others the assaults come from departmental faculty. In both cases the aim is to undermine the African American faculty's confidence, sense of collegiality, and intellectual integrity. We are targets of anti-African behavior at almost all levels of the university.

On the other hand, if our publications *are* credited to us then various indexes are checked to see how many times we are quoted by our peers. It is the old game of changing the rules to ensure our disadvantage. That is to say, and this really happened at the State University of New York at Albany, someone will want to examine the times an African American scholar was quoted by colleagues in order to determine if the person is significant enough to the white population to be hired. These types of interventions stem from the endemic nature of white supremacy, but they are not the most serious types of challenges. Despite the personal attacks on our scholars, the most insidious attack is the attempted intellectual assault on leading African American activist-intellectuals. In fact, since the Afrocentrists have argued that Egypt is as important to establishing a true intellectual genealogy of Africa as Greece is said to be to the same process in Europe, white scholars and some black scholars have come to challenge the Afrocentric view of society and education. They appear to find this quest as some sort of intellectual treason to the Western world. In addition to a line of African American neo-conservatives (Shelby Steele, Thomas Sowell, and Anne Wortham) and Euro-apologists (Michele Wallace and Henry L. Gates, Jr.), prominent white writers have given considerable space to attack the dynamic and positive idea of Afrocentric education, which says that African people must be viewed as subjects instead of objects.

Perhaps the crudest assault on African American scholarship came with the writing of an ideological tract by Arthur Schlesinger, Jr. Considered by white historians to be one of their most respected story-tellers, Schlesinger won Pulitzer Prizes for his books, *The Age of Jackson* (1945) and *A Thousand Days* (1965). These works, as well as his *Age of Roosevelt: the Imperial Presidency* and *Robert Kennedy and His Times,* established him as a leading American historian. Yet Schlesinger's recent book, *The Disuniting of America,* calls into question his understanding of American history and his appreciation of diversity. As a designated great American historian he is supposed to know something about what he writes. However, one of the most obvious manifestations of hegemonic thinking in cultural matters is pontification. Measuring the amount of pontification in *The Disuniting of America,* one comes away with a certain distrust of Schlesinger's writing as well as his perspective on the American society.[1] This is doubly so if one is an African American.

Schlesinger sets forth a vision of America rooted in the past, where whites, actually Anglo-Saxon whites, defined the protocols of the American society and white culture itself represented the ideal to which others were expected to aspire. He loves this vision because it provides a psychological justification for the dominance of European culture in America over others. In his vision there is little history of enslavement, oppression, dispossession, racism, or exploitation. In effect, there is no disunion in the Union; adjustments need to be made, for sure, but they are minor ripples in the perfect society. Fortunately, many whites as well as African Americans see this vision as corrupted by the arrogance of political, academic, and cultural dominance. How, they ask, can one have such a vision of America with what we know of our history? Yet this is Schlesinger's perspective on the American society as expressed in his most recent book.

Alas, the vision is clouded by Afrocentrists, the bad guys in Schlesinger's book, who bring disunity to this perfect world. Trapped in his own cultural prison, Schlesinger is unable to see the present American cultural reality and, I believe he has missed the point of the past as well. The evidence suggests that he holds a nearly static view of America. And perhaps the America of his youth—its academic life, social life, business environment, and political institutions—was framed for him in some version of the white American Dream. There is, of course, a nightmarish side to Schlesinger's vision or fantasy. He has peopled his vision with negations, colored by axioms that support no truth, but which are ultimately structured to uphold the status quo of white male privilege and domination. Had Schlesinger admitted this as a goal of his book, it would have allowed a more honest footing for discussion and debate. Nevertheless, this mixture of fact and fiction presents itself for analytical de-invention, not national disunity.

### Disunion and Disbelief
Of all the issues that might have grabbed Schlesinger's attention for disuniting America—unequal protection under the law, taxation without representation, gender strife, economic class

antagonisms, corrupt politicians, rampant anti-Africanism, growing anti-Semitism, pollution of the environment—he finds the African American challenge to the educational system a disuniting element, indeed, he believes it is a frightening development. Why should an Afrocentric position, that is, a position where Africans describe themselves as subjects rather than as objects, create such an uproar?

Are we to conclude that Schlesinger does not see the hegemonic imposition of the Eurocentric idea? Or do we conclude that he sees it and understands it and supports it? If he does not see it, then neither he nor others who believe as he does will understand the substance of what I am saying about symbolic, cultural, and economic domination and about resistance to intellectual imposition as necessary and liberating. Hegemonic thinking is like a person standing on the lid of a manhole. The fact that another person will rise out of that manhole means that the person standing on the lid will have to change positions or be toppled off. Will the Afrocentric perspective affect the Eurocentric hegemony on information and in education? Absolutely, because our perceptions are altered by new information, whether we admit it or not. A lifetime of delusion that denies Africans and Africa a place in human history creates a basic disbelief in facts that are presented in an Afrocentric framework. Indeed, Schlesinger's *The Age of Jackson* did not indicate any real appreciation for the nature of Jackson's racism and anti-Indian sentiments and practice. His glorification of Andrew Jackson, whom even Davy Crockett considered a scoundrel, is demonstrative of Schlesinger's disregard for the multi-ethnic, multi-cultural, pluralistic reality of the American society, past and present.

One must be factual and in trying to be factual I have always believed primary description is better than secondary interpretation. Thus, when Afrocentrists say that George Washington and Thomas Jefferson were slave-owners, *inter alia,* who did not believe in the equality of Africans, that is a descriptive fact of those two individuals. One can excuse the fact on grounds of interpretation, one can claim ignorance, one can argue that their good points outweighed their bad points, and so on; but the fact is that they believed in the inferiority of Africans. Students must be introduced to this factual information in order to make proper assessments and judgments. Schlesinger would insist that we not mention the racist heritage of the "founding fathers" because that would create disunity. If that be creating disunity, not only am I guilty as he claims in his book, but I will create more disunity because nothing is more valuable than the truth in bringing about true national integration.

Eurocentric control of space and time in publishing and the media has meant that legitimate intellectual and scholarly voices of African Americans are often not heard by whites who refuse to read African American scholarly journals. *The Journal of Black Studies, The Journal of Negro Education, The Journal of African Civilizations, Western Journal of Black Studies,* and *Imhotep* are a few of the prominent journals that are accessible to all scholars yet remain relatively unread by writers such as Schlesinger who apparently believe that there is little outside of the "white" journals worth reading. That is a serious mistake in scholarship, because reading the African American journals would greatly increase the appreciation for new findings and new ideas. Can Schlesinger really believe that only whites—or blacks who believe they are white—have reasonable ideas?

Afrocentrists, who get their degrees from the same institutions as white scholars, tend to have a far broader reading program that allows for more critical leverage to analysis. The fact that cyclopean stone tombs dating from 5700 B.C., among the earliest in the world, have been found in the heart of the Central African Republic may not be a part of one's knowledge base, but if it were known it would surely add to any discussion on historical time lines. Yet without reading any of my books or those of other Afrocentrists in depth, as far as I can discern, Schlesinger attempts to paint Afrocentrists as some

kind of wild bunch out to create disunity in the American society. What this celebrated white American historian seeks is
a dismissal of historical facts related to Africans as significant
in the American nation. He seems to operate within a closed
system of thought and such systems inevitably produce closed
minds. Education within such a system is found to produce
those who speak a certain restrictive language, use a handed-
down arcane political vocabulary, and believe in elves.

The danger, quite frankly, is that Schlesinger's attitude
toward difference itself *creates* insiders and outsiders—those
who are free to define themselves and others and those who
are the defined. There is no question in his mind about who
will do the defining. Afrocentrists flatly reject this kind of thinking and insist on defining our reality within the context of
society on the basis of agency.

To be Afrocentric is not to deny American citizenship.
Just as to be a Chinese American, live in Chinatown, employ
Chinese motifs in artistic expression, and worship Buddha is
not anti-American, the person who believes that the African
American must be re-centered, relocated in terms of historical referent (i.e., towards Africa) is not anti-American. This is
neither a destructive nor a disuniting behavior. It rather suggests the strengths of this country as compared with other
countries. The conviction that we will defend the rights of *all*
cultural expressions, not just Greco-Roman-Hebraic-Ger-
manic-Viking cultures, must be strongly embedded in our political psyches if the nation is to survive. In this way we avoid
what I call the Soviet problem which was the Russification of
the empire. Respect for each other's culture must be the guiding principle for a truly dynamic society. Since the American
idea is not a static but a dynamic one we must constantly re-
define ourselves in the light of our diverse experiences. One
reason this nation works the way it does is our diversity. Try
to make Africans and Asians copies of Europeans or women
copies of men and you will foster the disunity Schlesinger fears.
This does not mean, as some dishonest writers have written,

that black children will be taught black information and white children will be taught white information, and so forth. No Afrocentrist has articulated such a view though it has been widely reported in the news.

## UNITY IN AMERICA

The unity of America is based upon shared goals, a collective sense of mission, a common purpose, and mutual respect. It should be clear to the reader, upon reflection, that Schlesinger's view of America is too provincial, as if he has not escaped his 1945 vision when he wrote *The Age of Jackson*. I believe his view is planted in the narrow confines of a particular ethnic or racial identity. Thus it cannot produce a harvest of unity. The unity of the American nation is not a unity of historical experiences or of cultural backgrounds. Because each of us could give a different version of the same story, there must be an acceptance of pluralism without ethnic or cultural hegemony. Only in this manner can we build a common culture. For the present we have many co-cultures, occasionally interacting with each other, but we have only one society. This means that it is no longer viable for German, English, French, Italian, Greek, or Armenian cultures to parade as the exclusive definition of American culture.

## ON MULTICULTURALISM

I find it curious that Schlesinger, who has spent a lifetime championing an elitist educational program, is now interested in a multicultural one. This may be a result of his professorship at City University of New York or the controversy surrounding a number of his colleagues at the City University. I should not be mistaken. I like the idea that Schlesinger sees multiculturalism as important; it is just that he would be the last person I would consider knowledgeable of this field.

There is no particularist multiculturalism or pluralist multiculturalism; there is quite simply, multiculturalism. I pointed out in response to Diane Ravitch, who first came up with the notions of particularist and pluralist multiculturalisms that the first is an oxymoron and the second a redundancy. Multiculturalism is not a complicated proposition; it is clear and simple. In a multicultural society there must be a multicultural curriculum, a multicultural approach to institution-building, and so forth.[2]

Afrocentrists say that one should not be able to declare competency in music in America without having been introduced to the Spirituals, Duke Ellington, or the Blues. Yet every year students graduate with degrees in music who have never been introduced to the Spirituals and it only happens in major American universities because of an Eurocentric orientation to all knowledge.

## AN AFROCENTRIC ORIENTATION

What Schlesinger dislikes in the Afrocentric position is the emphasis on re-centering of African Americans in a subject position *vis*-à-*vis* history, culture, and science. However, 380 years of white domination have disoriented, dislocated, and displaced many African Americans. This is the legacy of stealing us from Africa, dehumanizing us, and enslaving us. So fearful of Africans were the slave masters that they sought to rob us of our heritage, memory, languages, religion, customs, traditions, and history. In the end, it is true, some of us did lose our way and our minds and some of us would claim that we came over to America on *The Mayflower*. They are de-centered and disoriented and often alienated; Afrocentricity seeks to understand this phenomenon by beginning all analysis from the African person as human agent. In classes, it means that the African American child must be connected, grounded to information presented in the same way white children are grounded when we discuss literature, history, mathematics, and science. Teachers who do not know this information with respect to Africans must seek it out from those who do know it. Afrocentrists do not take anything away from white history except its aggressive urge to pose as universal.

The meaning of this school of thought is critical for all Americans. I make a claim that we must see ourselves within the American society with points of reference to our own ancestral culture and history. Our children as well as other children must know about us in the context of our own history. The Afrocentric school of thought becomes useful for the expansion of dialogue and the widening of our discourse— the proper function of education. The white self-esteem curriculum now present in most school systems is imposed as universal. Of course, we know it is not universal but specific social studies and humanities information centered on a particular culture. There is nothing fundamentally wrong about a Eurocentric curriculum so long as other cultures are not denied; that is, so long as it is not a hegemonic Eurocentrism. The real question is whether Eurocentrism can exist without denial of the other? To speak arrogantly of this model as a conquest model is to assert a claim of right by force not on the basis of facts nor on the grounds of what is useful for this society. We ought to be able to develop a curriculum of instruction that affirms all people in their cultural heritages.

## A Finished Paradigm

It is bizarre to find that Schlesinger attacks my vision of a multicultural nation without having read any of my works. At the end of the twentieth century the United States must be spared the intellectual intolerance, xenophobia, ethnic hatred, racist thinking, and hegemonic attitudes that now seem to be running rampant in the European continent.

Schlesinger seeks to divide African American intellectuals into two camps in order to bash Afrocentrists. There are women who accept the male view of history. There were Jews who accepted the German version of culture. There will always be members of the dominated group who will accept certain ideas from those dominating. We all experience our particular dislocations. But for me, an American citizen of African descent, I shall never abandon my ancestors' history. Neither would I expect Schlesinger to abandon his, though that is his right. Whether he accepts it or abandons it, I will not say he is sowing disunity.

Dividing African scholars in order to foment conflict is an old game, but it avoids raising the issue discussed by the Afrocentrists. Why should a monocultural experience and history dominate a multicultural and multiethnic nation? There is no good answer to this question, so Schlesinger believes in shoring up the old "perfect" order as the best procedure. But it will not wash. His description is of a paradigm that is finished. It is not enough for Schlesinger to cite majority support, since popular belief and mass acceptance are not adequate for validating ideas. Description and demonstration are the principal calling cards of proof, not authoritative pronouncements, even if they come from a well-known historian. Neither hegemony nor power can determine truth.

## NATIONALITY AND CULTURE

Schlesinger's book is unfortunate at this stage in national integration and development. He confuses American nationality with American culture. Whether by choice or circumstances we are American in citizenship. So one can argue that my nationality and citizenship are American even while my historical and cultural origins are African. My ancestors did not arrive in this country from Europe. They did not see a mountain of possibility in this land, but rather a valley of despair.

It is this distinction, this historical cleavage that cannot be resolved by some mythical idea that we all came here on the *Mayflower.* The preferred resolution of such dual experiences is a true multiculturalism, where Europeans are seen working for a national purpose *alongside* of other people, not in an hegemonic position. This takes a measure of humility which is not evident in Schlesinger's book. However, without a re-orientation from conquest, from dominance, from superiority, the whites in this country can never understand the discourse of unity expressed by Africans, Latinos, Asians, and Native Americans.

I agree with President Franklin Roosevelt's observation that "Americanism is not a matter of race and ancestry but of adherence to the creed of liberty and democracy." This means that the litmus test for Americanism must not be how Eurocentric a person becomes, but whether the person adheres to the common American project. One cannot construe a Chinese American's love of Chinese motifs, history, decorations, and myths as a rejection of Americanism; it *is* Americanism. Of course, we all are free to reject our ethnic or cultural past but that does not mean we do not possess culture.

### Fashioning the Enemy

Schlesinger writes in a very condescending manner:

> Nor is there anything more natural than for generous-hearted people, black and white, to go along with Afrocentrism out of a decent sympathy for the insulted and injured of American society and of a decent concern to bind up the wounds. (73)

But Afrocentricity is not about sympathy or insult; it is about the proper presentation of factual information in a multicultural society. To frame an argument in the context of the generous-hearted doing something for Africans is to miss the point. What we do by making America safe for diversity is to ensure the unity of the nation. Schlesinger's line of thinking suggests that his condescension is unabated:

> Still, doctrinaire ethnicity in general and the dog-
> matic black version in particular raise questions
> that deserve careful and dispassionate examina-
> tion. (73-74)

This is a representation of the Afrocentric movement that seeks to diminish that movement's rational arguments by hyperbole. Doctrinaire ethnicity, if it exists in America, is not to be found in the African American community if one examines any sector of the society. Schlesinger is especially exercised by "the dogmatic black version"—which he does not describe in any detail—Yet he says that the Afrocentric campaign most worries him. His problem with Afrocentric scholarship is that he cannot dismiss it. For example, he wants to question the African origin of civilizaton and counterposes Mesopotamia as the cradle of civilization. But this does not work either in theory or reality.

## THE AFRICAN ORIGIN OF CIVILIZATION

Cheikh Anta Diop wrote in *The African Origin of Civilization* that Africa is the cradle of human civilization. He expanded his argument in his massive work, *Civilization and Barbarism*, assembling evidence from disparate sources such as linguistics, botany, osteology, history, and molecular biology.[3] Numerous scholars have supported the arguments made by Diop in those books. In fact, Theophile Obenga has shown the origin of medicine, theology, queenship, astronomy, mathematics, ethics, and philosophy in Africa. There is no comparable evidence of antiquity in any other continent.[4]

Mesopotamia does not figure in ancient civilization, either concretely or philosophically, at the same level as ancient Egypt. Even were one to take evidence from the ancient Egyptian, Hebrew, Greek, and Ethiopian people, one would find that the Nile Valley of Africa rather than the Tigris-Euphrates Valley was considered the most ancient cradle of human civilization.

Plato's corpus includes 28 extant dialogues. In twelve of those dialogues he discusses Egypt, not Mesopotamia, Sumer, or Babylon. Of course, Plato himself was taught in Africa by Seknoufis and Kounoufis. He did not think of Mesopotamia as a high civilization of the level of Egypt. The Hebrew Bible mentions Egypt nearly one thousand times, Mesopotamia no more than twenty. The Ethiopians refer to Egypt, not to Mesopotamia, in their ancient sacred books *Kebra Nagast* and *The Book of Henok.* While I believe Mesopotamia was a significant civilization, I also believe that it is advanced as a sort of contemporary anti-African project, a kind of counterpoint to the African origin of civilization. This is why some writers claim that Mesopotamian civilization can be dated one hundred years prior to the First Egyptian Dynasty. However, dynastic Egypt was not the beginning of civilization in the Nile Valley. There had been at least sixteen kings of Upper (Southern) Egypt before Narmer (Menes), who is normally given as the first dynastic king. My point is that neither the ancient Nubians, Greeks, nor Hebrews considered Mesopotamia more important than Egypt; this idea of Mesopotamia's place alongside Egypt is pre-eminently a contemporary (i.e., modern) project.

Let us examine Schlesinger's assault on the Egyptian scholarship of African scholars. He admits that he is no expert on ancient Egypt and in a broad stroke for justification claims "neither are the educators and psychologists who push Afrocentrism." I do not know what special criteria Schlesinger is using for expertise, but Cheikh Anta Diop, Theophile Obenga, Wade Nobles, Maulana Karenga, Asa Hilliard, and others have spent more than one hundred collective years in the study of ancient Africa. Their research and publications are accessible and well-known to those of us who consider ourselves Afrocentrists. All of these scholars are students of ancient languages, Medu Netcher (the language of the ancient Egyptians), Ge'ez ("classical" Ethiopians), Greek, and Latin. Although my knowledge of the ancient language is not

nearly at the level of the scholars I have mentioned, my familiarity with the ancient literatures is indicated in many of the
books that I have written. My book, *Kemet, Afrocentricity,
and Knowledge*, for instance, explores various aspects of the
historiography of ancient Africa.

Schlesinger's attack seeks to undermine the Africanness
of the ancient Egyptian. Indeed he brings three witnesses to
his case: Frank Snowden, Frank Yurco, and Miriam Lichtheim.
All three of these people have deeply invested interests in the
Eurocentric paradigm of history, that is, the projection of
Eurocentric concepts on African people. Snowden, a retired
Howard University professor, has written on the African image in Greece and Rome. He does not read Medu Netcher
and certainly is no scholar of ancient Africa. Yurco, a librarian
at the University of Chicago, has produced nothing of the caliber of any of the Afrocentrists. He remains a sort of front man
for the Aryan construction of the Egyptological field. From
his Regenstein Library desk at the University of Chicago,
Yurco's career rests on responding to Diop, Bernal, Hilliard,
and lately my own, *Kemet, Afrocentricity, and Knowledge.*
His ideological perspective appears to fog his analysis. His
essay *Biblical Archaeological Review,* cited by Schlesinger,
is a nasty little piece written against Martin Bernal.

Miriam Lichtheim is by far the best known ancient Egyptian scholar, but the comment Schlesinger chooses to use from
Lichtheim is rather strange. She is quoted as saying:

> I do not wish to waste any of my time refuting the
> errant nonsense which is being propagated in the
> American black community about the Egyptians
> being Nubians and the Nubians being black. The
> Egyptians were not Nubians, and the original
> Nubians were not black. Nubia gradually became
> black because black peoples migrated northward
> out of Central Africa. The "Nile Valley School" is
> obviously an attempt by American blacks to pro-

vide themselves with an ancient history linked to
that of the high civilization of ancient Egypt. (77)

Nothing could contain as much "errant nonsense" as this statement. I do not know anyone claiming that the ancient Egyptians and Nubians represented the same country; they did represent the same race of people. The Egyptians and the Nubians *were* the same people in the same sense that the Germans and the Dutch are the same people. They have different nationalities and histories, but they are more like each other than either one is like the Amhara of Ethiopia.

Neither Schlesinger nor Lichtheim name or quote any African or African American scholar as saying anything "about the Egyptians being Nubians." However, let me reiterate that the difference between Nubians and Egyptians was much like that of Sicilians and Italians, Icelanders and Danes, or Germans and Austrians. Lichtheim's comment and Schlesinger's use of it is meant to suggest that the ancient Egyptians and ancient Nubians were of different races. Nubians and Egyptians, however, looked alike and came from the same general culture. In addition, they were both black-skinned people.

Lichtheim's denial of the blackness, (that is, the black-skinnedness) of the ancient Nubians borders on intellectual incompetence because it disregards the available concrete evidence in texts, sculptures, paintings, and linguistics. Lichtheim's statement that the "Egyptians were not Nubians" is technically correct, but is effectually misleading. One can say that the French are not Spanish or the Swedes are not Norwegians, but that is not a statement about the color of skin. I can say that the Yoruba are not Ibo and that tells me something about ethnicity and perhaps national identity, but not about their complexions. So, to say that the Egyptians were not Nubians is to say no more than that the two people who lived along the Nile occupied different geographical areas.

The fact is that the Egyptians saw themselves and Nubians as looking exactly alike in physical appearance as well as dress.

One only needs to know the depiction of ethnology in the world, the Biban el-Moluk bas relief from the tomb of Sesostris I, to see that Egyptians painted themselves and Nubians as coal black, and whites and Asians as lighter in complexion. In addition there is the ethnology from the period of Rameses III, the 12th century B.C.E., which demonstrates further the extent to which the Egyptians saw themselves as black-skinned people. There are four people in the painting representing four different cultures: Remetiu (Egyptian), Nehasu (Nubian), Namou (Semite), and Tamhou (Libyan)). The Egyptian and the Nubian are exactly alike, even to their clothes. They are visibly different from the Namou and the Tamhou.

But the greater nonsense is Lichtheim's statement that the "original Nubians were not black." Does Lichtheim mean to imply that they were what we would call white today? Does she mean they were lighter complexioned blacks? Or does she mean to suggest, as some white Egyptologists suggested in the past, that the people were "black-skinned whites"? The problem here is racialist thinking. Since the discourse under which white academics have often operated is Eurocentric, it is difficult for them to admit that civilization not only started in Africa but that it was black people who started it.

As far as we know at the present, human beings originated on the African continent and migrated outward. No scientist suggests that the people who migrated outward and who peopled the continent of Africa were white. Indeed, the monogenesis thesis argues that a group of hominids called the Grimaldi migrated to Europe and emerged from the post-Wurm Ice Age as white in complexion due to environmental and climatic factors.

The Nubians were not only black physically, but shared with the Egyptians and others of the Nile Valley the same African cultural and philosophical modalities. Present-day Egypt, like present-day America, is not a reflection of its ancient past. Arabs came from Arabia with the jihads of the 7th Century

C.E. Therefore, Arabic is not indigenous to Africa as English is not indigenous to the United States.

The aim of Schlesinger's remarks and Lichtheim's quote is not the Nubian issue but the question of the complexion of the ancient Egyptians. Afrocentrists claim that Eurocentric scholars have attempted to take Egypt out of Africa and to take Africans out of ancient Egypt by a process of whitening the earliest civilizations. Children's books still exist with Egyptians looking like Scandinavians.

The evidence of the blackness of the ancient Egyptians is overwhelming. The early Greeks said that the Egyptians were black. They never wrote that the Egyptians were white. In fact, Aristotle wrote in *Physiognomonica* that both the Egyptians and the Ethiopians (Nubians) were black. Herodotus writes in *The Histories* that the people of Colchis (an ancient region corresponding to the present-day Georgian Republic) must be Egyptians because "like them they have black skin and wooly hair."[5] One could cite Strabo, Pindar, and Appollonius of Rhodes as making similar attestations about how the Egyptians looked to them.

Thus, Lichtheim's statement is not only errant, but is itself pure nonsense. It flies in the face of all available evidence, and beyond that it defies logic. Perhaps this style of pontification by white scholars is the source of confusion in the minds of the American public. Lichtheim proposes what Martin Bernal has aptly called the Aryan Model of Ancient History, which suggests, among other things, that civilization *could not* have started in Africa and if civilization *is* found in Africa it had to be the result of an external movement *into* Africa. This is a racist construction of the origin of African civilizations that seeks to deny African capability.

## E Pluribus Unum

Schlesinger likes to quote Diane Ravitch. But both Schlesinger and Ravitch are wrong when they suggest that *E Pluribus*

*Unum* meant out of many cultures, one. Actually this expression was initially applied to the fact that several colonies could produce one federal government. Thus, out of many colonies, one central government. To apply this term of political structure to the American cultural reality is to miss the point of both politics and culture. A nation of more than 130 cultural groups cannot hope to have all of them Anglo-Saxonized. Such a vision is disastrous and myopic. What we can aim for—and realize—is a society of mutual respect, dynamism, and decency. Rather than pitting cultural groups against each other, or labeling them, we should empower a vision which sees the American kaleidiscope of cultures as uniquely fortunate.

Schlesinger, gravely, sees multiculturalism as a danger. I see it as a further indication that the shift to a new, more operable paradigm is well underway and that we will soon be able to move in this new direction with a more human commitment to communality.

# 3

## FOUNDATIONS FOR AFRICAN INTELLECTUAL AGENCY AND EUROPEAN RESISTANCE

In the West, almost all the knowledge about Africa is Eurocentric, that is, it has been mediated or delivered by white Westerners for the purpose of fitting Africa into the European world. It could be Rattray's Ghana or Breasted's Egypt or Lady Lugard's Nigeria or Tempel's Central Africa, but everywhere it is the same story. In the Islamic world, the image of Africa and Africans has similarly been viewed through the lenses of the Arab world. It is as if there has been no voice of Africa itself, free of external intervention. Is this once more the notion of Africa as pupil and outsiders as teachers? Even in Africa itself we are often confronted with the same structure of knowledge, often to such an absurd degree that in one textbook in Nigeria there is the statement by a Nigerian that the Scot, Mungo Park discovered the Niger River. Of course, Africans led Park to the river bank. Perhaps because the great Arabic intervention preceded the European intervention, it has become much more absorbed into the real flesh of the people. Both interventions, however, have dislocated much of the original tissue of the intellectual and cultural life of the continent.

The West is a euphemism in most cases for European or European-dominated thought; it rarely refers to the indigenous or previously enslaved peoples who may also find themselves in the West.[1] Yet, as you full well know, I am not saying that some of these Native American people and African people in the Americas do not claim to be Western; they do. In the United States, we have a considerable number of them now declaring in no uncertain terms that their indigenous status or their previously enslaved position has been wiped out completely and that they are now Westerners. Or we now find Africans claiming to be Europeans in their outlook. And, indeed, if they say they are, then in their minds and bodies they probably are. So the West remains a euphemism, but a euphemism for the complete obliteration of other ways of knowing and the domination of a particularism, that is, a particular human perspective on the world, as if it were universal. The implications for knowledge in this case are tremendous; the combination of power, parades, and propaganda supporting this particularism creates a virtual reality from which it is hard to discern the real from the unreal.

A number of African scholars have now deciphered the lessons of history and explicated the fundamental characteristics of the hold that the West has on the rest of us. The cultural hold that the West has exerted on Africa since the fifteenth century has been reinforced by the impact of the enslavement of Africans, by the Grand Army's invasion of Africa in 1798, and by the Berlin Conference of 1884-85.

The Europeans did not discuss with Africans the dividing-up (between theselves) of the continent; they simply divided it up. Then they had the audacity to write about their control of the territory. They wrote what they wanted, interpreted as they pleased, and made their explanations of African history and culture the received ones. The colonization was not only of land, but of culture as well.

Of course there is nothing wrong with Europeans writing about Africa or taking an interest in Africa or African people;

it represents an important continent in the origin of the human race and the people of Africa constitute modern man's first encounter with hominids in the form of *australopithecus ramidus* and *australopithecus afarensis* as well as the earliest human civilizations. Indeed, the earliest philosophers we have any record of in the world are black African philosophers. Here, like Cheikh Anta Diop and Theophile Obenga, I use "black" for emphasis, since some might admit they were African but not black.

The problem of knowledge regarding Africa is that too many of the Europeans who have written of Africa have had the European project of white domination, of white power, of white race supremacy at the very top of their agenda in the explanations and interpretations of phenomena they saw or information they were given. Thus, in the West, Africans themselves have often remained outside of the standard interpretations of data about Africa or Africans. Some European writers such as Stephen Howe have tried to make a distinction between continental and diasporan Africans in terms of the problem of knowledge. They assert that the continental Africans do not raise the same questions as African Americans regarding identity and history. What they do not understand is that continental and diasporan Africans, when confronted with the facts, are on the same page about the necessity for Afrocentricity. This is so, despite the fact that we have different specific histories. Fortunately, it is no longer possible for Europeans to interpret the African's world for their own interests without the utter involvement of Africans on both sides of the Atlantic.

I shall attempt to show how we can navigate through the difficulties imposed by the European structure of knowlege. But first it is necessary that I recite the background to this present situation.

Late in the eighteenth century, at the University of Göttingen, Wilhelm von Humboldt and Alexander von Humboldt began to develop the racial hierarchical theories that would catapult European thought into the next centuries as the watchdogs of truth. The intention of the Humboldts and other European writers and promoters was the creation of a world in which the dominant motifs of thought and behavior would reflect the European world. Not unlike the conquest of territory that had begun in the fifteenth century, this information conquest would prove to be just as important in the construction of the West.

So aggressive would these early propaganda tycoons be in promoting their ideology that they would not only conjoin it with capitalism and imperialism but would spread it to other parts of the world and convince many Africans and Asians that Europeans and European culture not only were superior but they were destined to be superior.

European scientists, scholars, men and women of learning would propagate the most abhorrent nonsense about race. So-called biologists, physiologists, and medical doctors would advance theories about brain size, penis size, and head bones to demonstrate their points about white supremacy. This would become the background stuff for much of Western theorizing about the world. Movies would be made, theater plays written, essays disseminated, and sermons preached proclaiming a sort of manifest destiny for the white race.

Make no mistake, what we have today in every sector—art, education, economics, law, medicine—is the legacy of five hundred years of Western promotion of this ideology of European supremacy. It structures everything—not simply in Western countries, but increasingly in other countries where Westerners have exported the ideology of hierarchical racial thinking.

Recently at my university, the Dean of the College of Arts and Sciences proposed a new department, to be a combination of the old French, German, Italian, and Spanish departments. She announced the intention to name it the Department of Modern Languages. This, I suppose, is an acceptable view in a virtual Eurocentric world, however false. A more correct and appropriate title would have been Department of Modern *European* Languages. To create a title which ignores the rest of the world's "modern" languages and to appropriate the term for European hegemony is another tactic in the promotion of white supremacy. The madness is that our own African universities often promote the same agenda. It is almost as if Westerners and Africans have been on the same "automatic pilot" in this regard. But, of course, that is not the case; Western history is richly furbished with character witnesses to the ideological project.

Most modern museums make a great separation of Egyptian Art from African Art. In fact, I have visited many of the world's great museums and have spoken at quite a few where this construction had been enshrined in some nineteenth-century notion of hierarchy and domination. To separate Ancient Egypt from the rest of Africa is like separating Ancient Greece or Rome from the rest of Europe.

It must be restated that racist categories and classifications were not the creation of African intellectuals. This was left to the Europeans who had their own axe to grind in the area of racial hierarchies. In the Netherlands during the eighteenth-century, Peter Campier (1722-1789) compared African facial and skull measurements to those of monkeys and developed a racial hierarchy in which he claimed that Greek statuary was the highest form of human aesthetics and that the lowest form was the image of the African. Campier and his colleagues had a profound impact on the thinking of the West in regards to African art.

We must be careful to say that racist thinking was not the undertaking of every white writer. Actually, racist ideology was formed by a narrow group of clergymen, philosophers, curators, physicians, and scientists who lived on the salaries of churches, museums, and universities. These were the spreaders of racial exclusivity, the bishops of racial hierarchy, and the evangelists of white supremacy.

Many had never seen an African or been to Africa. And those who had, often formed their opinions before ever encountering Africa. Widely differing accounts of Africans often emerged from white travellers to the continent. For example, Count Constantin de Volney, a Frenchman (1757-1820), travelled to Egypt in the eighteenth century *prior to* the invasion of the French Army and claimed in his book *Ruins of Empire,* (1791) that Europe owed its arts, civilizations, and sciences to  Africans. "Just think that this race of black men, today our slave and the object of our scorn, is the very race to which we owe our arts, sciences, and even the use of Speech!"[1] But Volney was  the exception in a long line of racist thinkers.

David Hume, for instance, in 1748 wrote "I am apt to suspect that the Negroes in general are naturally inferior to whites. There has never  been a civilized nation of any other complexion than white."

George Cuvier, called the Aristotle of his age, the founder of geology, paleontology, and comparative anatomy, wrote in his major 16-volume work, *The Animal Kingdom,* in 1812 that the "African is the most degraded of human races and whose form approaches that of the beast and whose intelligence is no where great enough to arrive at regular governance."

Georg Hegel, the greatest European thinker of his century, wrote in 1828 "Let us forget Africa never to return to it for Africa is no part of the historical globe, it is outside of history."

Louis Agassiz, the Harvard naturalist of the nineteenth century, wrote "This compact continent of Africa exhibits a population which has enjoyed the example of Egypt but nevertheless there has never been a regulated form of government on that continent."

"I advance it therefore, as a suspicion only, that the blacks, whether originally a distinct race or made distinct by time and circumstance, are inferior to the whites in the endowments of both body and mind," said Thomas Jefferson in his *Notes on Virginia* in 1790.

Arnold Toynbee the English historian wrote that "Of the 21 great civilizations of the world, not one has been produced in Africa."

Ulrich Phillips wrote that "the Negro was what the white man made him...the traits which prevailed were an eagerness in society, music, merriment, a fondness for display whether of person, dress, vocabulary, or emotion, a not flagrant sensuality, a receptiveness toward any religion whose exercises were exhilarating, a proneness to superstition, a courteous acceptance of subordination, an avidity for praise, a readiness for loyalty of a feudal sort, and a repugnance toward overwork."

Numerous famous European writers have betrayed their hatred, disdain, or prejudice against Africa and Africans. In fact, Marvin Harris, in his study of anthropology's roots, shows that the giants of that field with the exception of two were racists against Africans.

It is only in this light that we can adequately frame the discussion about Afrocentricity, whether philosophical or cultural. Early Africa stands at the door of knowledge in the modern world. Africa taught Europe in geometry, medicine, astronomy, philosophy, and literature. Africa was often the source and the method by which Europe gained its information. Papyrus, from which we get the word paper, is native to Africa. Indeed, when Amr conquered Egypt in 639 C.E. he set up the potential for African ideas and influences, from architecture to philosophy, from mathematics to science, to be spread over the globe with the spreading of the prophet's faith.

Thus, it is important to dispel myths in order to be able to see that the demonology practiced against Afrocentrists is another attempt to advance a racial or cultural hierarchical agenda.

Frederick Douglass, in a letter to his son in 1887 while visiting Egypt, wrote, "It has been the fashion of American writers, to deny that the Egyptians were Negroes and claim that they are of the same race as themselves. This has, I have no doubt, been largely due to a wish to deprive the Negro of the moral support of Ancient Greatness and to appropriate the same to the white race.[2]

So poisoned is the water of Africa's early history that it will take an entirely new Afrocentrically trained cadre of scholars to purify the work of the racist Egyptologists, philosophers, and anthropologists whose only ambition, it seemed, was to claim racial pre-eminence of white people. Thus, for example, someone like J. E. Manchip White, an archaeologist, writes of Pharaoh Piankhi who preferred his capital city of Napata to Thebes that the Nubians felt "ill-at-ease among the fair-skinned Egyptians"[3] as if the conquerors were overwhelmed by the whiteness of the Egyptians and, even though they had conquered Egypt, fled back to Napata, the capital city. Never would he think of saying that when Alexander conquered Persia he fled back to Greece rather than remain in Persia because he felt ill at ease among the Persians.

Yet White is a lightweight in the attempt to locate a white race in Africa. Yet White is influenced enough by the racism of the West to write this following nonsense: "The civilization of Lower Egypt (Northern Egypt) was almost certainly more advanced...than the civilization of Upper Egypt (Southern Egypt.)"[4] This was certainly not the case. Contrary evidence exists not simply in the literature but in the land itself. More than half of the monuments of Egypt are located in the area surrounding the southern city of ancient Thebes (Luxor). Actually the evidence suggests that civilization came from the South upper Egypt and spread to the North (Lower Egypt), just as the first dynastic king, Menes or Narmer, came from the South. But White in his ethereal reasoning is not to be satisfied (he cannot be satisfied, because he knows his argument makes little sense), so in order to try to buttress it he calls on even more nonsense, such as: "It is indisputable that Asian ideas were reaching Upper Egypt."[5] There is every reason to dispute his construction of the facts and far more reason to question his motives. Expressions like "It appears clear" or "Certainly, we must accept"or "there seems little doubt" suggest that it is not clear and there is every doubt.

How to declare the black people of Egypt white was a haunting problem in the minds of racist white Egyptologists such as Budge, Breasted, Reisner, Lepsius, and Maspero. They all attempted to make their cases on the basis of the superiority of the white race. They became the mainstream thinkers in this field, the ones referred to by those who want to claim that the Egyptians were whites. James Breasted in his major work, *The Conquest of Civilization,* written in 1926, declared that Egypt was part of the Orient, a term which had gained favor in the West with the Arab conquest of Egypt and the subsequent domination by the Ottoman Turks.[6] Of course, we all know, as Breasted knew, that Ancient Egypt existed thousands of years before Islam and that the Arabs and Turks had no part in the ancient history of Egypt, except as the Asiatics referred to *by* the Ancient Egyptians.

This idea of Oriental Culture, largely refers to a movement around Islamic cultures: Turkey, Persia, Syria, and Iraq. To claim Egypt for the so-called Orient is to take it out of the continent of Africa. One of Breasted's chapters is called "Western Asia: The Scene of the Evolution of Civilization and the Great White Race." But for him, Western Asia was clearly North Africa. Although for Breasted the Egyptians were dark-skinned, they could still be referred to as white because they had other indicators of intelligence, and as he believed only whites could create civilization. Sir Gaston Maspero, who was director of antiquities at the Cairo Museum under British rule, wrote that the Egyptians "were black skinned whites." Other whites would claim that they discovered "white" skulls in prehistoric East Central Africa. This was actually claimed in 1959 by Harvard anthropologist William Howells. Physical anthropology has not been able to precisely assign racial labels to skeletal remains of early hominids. This remains an inexact science. What we can now discuss is the significance of dioxyribonucleic acid's structure in the genealogy of humans. Of course this awareness and science came much later than the writings of the early European Egyptologists.

Breasted, the founder of the Oriental Institute, would take racism further and write: "On the south of the Northwest Quadrant lay the teeming black world of Africa, separated from the Great White Race by an impassable desert barrier, the Sahara, which forms so large a part of the Southern Flatlands. Isolated thus and at the same time unfitted by ages of tropical life for any effective intrusion among the White Race the negro (sic) and negroid (sic) peoples remained without any influence on the development of early civilization. We may then exclude both of these external races—the straight-haired, round-headed, yellow-skinned Mongoloids on the east, and the wooly-haired, long-headed, dark-skinned Negroids on the South—from any share in the origins (or) subsequent development of civilization."[7]

In a highly contradictory passage, Charles Seignobos, a French scholar, wrote in his *History of Ancient Civilization* that "Almost all civilized peoples belong to the white race. The people of other races have remained savage or barbarian....It is within the limits of Asia and Africa that the first civilized peoples had their development—the Egyptians in the Nile Valley, the Chaldeans in the plains of the Euphrates....Their skin was dark, the hair short and thick, the lips strong. Nobody knows their origin with exactness and scholars are not agreed on the name to give them."[8]

One only has to turn to the ancients themselves to see the truth of the matter. The name of the early civilizers was known by the ancients. In fact, Diodorus Siculus, in his *On Egypt* in the first century before Christ, says that many persons of Greek ancestry who are "celebrated among the Greeks for intelligence and learning, ventured to Egypt in olden times, that they might partake of the customs and sample the teaching there. For the priests of the Egyptians cite from the records in their holy books, that in former times they were visited by Orpheus and Musaeus, Melampos and Daedalos, besides the poet Homer. Lycurgus, the Spartan, Solon the Athenian, and Plato the philosopher. Pythagoras of Samos and the mathematician Eudoxos, as well as Democritus of Abdera and Oenopides of Chios, also came there."[9]

But Diodorus is only one of more than ten Greek and Roman writers who attest to the contributions of Africa to the Greeks through ancient Egypt. In fact, Diodorus is very explicit that Homer even went to Egypt for opium to banish his pain and sorrow. The drug nepenthic, a type of opium or hashish, which he obtained from Thebes was used to get rid of depression.[10]

Most Greeks, however, went to study in Egypt, not to find drugs. "Lycurgos, as well as Solon and Plato, are reported to have inserted many of the Egyptian customs into their own codes of law, while Pythagoras, they say, learned from the Egyptians the doctrine of divine wisdom, the theorems of geometry, the theory of numbers, and in addition, the transmigration of the soul into every living being."[11] In addition, we learn that Democritus learned many of the secrets of astrology from the Egyptians during a five-year stay in Africa. But he was not alone in this line of study; Oenopides was also a disciple of the priests in astrology and astronomy. He learned about the sun and the stars. In like manner, Eudoxos studied astronomy with the Egyptians and transmitted much information to Greece, acquiring a reputation for knowledge. Sculptors such as Telecles and Theodoros, sons of Rhoecos, the most renowned Greek sculptors of their day, learned what they knew about proportions for a statue from following the Egyptian pattern of dividing the scale of the complete body into twenty-one and a quarter units and having sculptors to work on their own portions and once they have finished they complete the project by fitting the pieces together.

Herodotus in a similar vein, about four hundred years earlier, says:

Egyptians were the first of mankind to invent the year
and make twelve divisions of the seasons for it. They
said that this invention of the year was based on the
stars. Their reckoning, in my opinion, is much clev-
erer than that of the Greeks: for the Greeks must insert
one intercalary month (because of taking account of
the seasons) every other year, but the Egyptians, by
allotting thirty days apiece to each of the twelve months
(and adding five days outside of the number in each
year), make the cycle of the seasons come out to the
same point as the calendar. These authorities also say
that the Egyptians were the first to use the names of
the twelve gods, and that the Greeks took these from
them, and that the Egyptians were the first to assign
altars and images and temples to the gods and to carve
figures of stone.[12]

Herodotus also informs us that the "names of nearly all the
gods came from Egypt to Greece."[13]

The African philosophers who predate the first Greek philosopher Thales (600 B.C. E.) include Khunanup, Ptahhotep,
Pepi I, Khety, Kagemni, and Amenhotep, the Son of Hapu.
The teachers of Plato include Khnouphis and Seknouphis, the
teacher of Solon was Sochis, and one of the teachers of
Pythagoras was Wennofer. The earliest record of philosophy
as a concept is on an inscription on the tomb of Antef I from
2052 B.C., in Africa, not in Asia nor in Europe or North
America.

Another line of argument that is often used to deprive
Africa of its own historic past is to divide Africans into those
who are not purely Africans and those who are. The common
determiner seems to be what some writers call "the white qualities." Thus, Lady Lugard in *A Tropical Dependency* says that
the Fulani, Hausa, and the Songhay people, "though black,
are absolutely distinct from the pure Negro type."[14] What this
means has escaped me ever since I first read it. These pure
Negro types are never clearly defined, because there are no

such people in Africa. There are various ethnic groups, linguistic groups, none of which answers by the title of Negro. This "pure Negro type" was a creation of the white imagination that defied definition in any objective sense. On the east side of Africa, Osgood claimed in 1928 that the Ethiopians were not indigenous to Africa. Of course there are at least 20 different ethnic groups of Ethiopians, the Oromo being the largest. Nevertheless, he writes: "The Ethiopian is by no means a Negro. He is dark-skinned, with hair usually kinky and lips frequently thick, but he has a good high-bridged nose, well-set eyes, and a firm chin. To this he adds a proud and dignified bearing and a warlike, patriotic spirit."[15] Now we know, it is his warlike and patriotic spirit that separates the Ethiopian from other Africans, since the physical characteristics of Africans are as varied as the people. We have no explanation for other African peoples who also have martial and patriotic traditions. Some other trait must make them African since they may, as the Asante and Zulu demonstrate, have long traditions of military organization.

Other writers have argued the peculiar view that the Masai and Watutsi are really not African because their bearing is much too proud to be African. Why is it that there are so many Africans in Africa who are not really African, but no Europeans in Europe who are not European?

What seems to be disturbing a number of traditional Egyptologists and historians now is the fact that scholars in the Association for the Study of Classical African Civilizations and the Association for Nubian and Kemetic Heritage are now debunking much of the racist construction of ancient African history. This is particularly true in the case of the Ancient Egyptians. Since the nineteenth century the West has tried to appropriate Egypt as a part of the West and not a part of Africa. Clearly this is not about physical territory, since all you have to do is to look at a map and you will see that Egypt is in Africa. On the other hand, this is a story of *intellectual* territory. The early Egyptologists, in the nineteenth and twenieth centuries, knew that Egypt was the greatest and most majestic civilization of antiquity and they sought to adopt it for their own ancient, though remote origins. This is fine, but in doing so they did something else which, in their racist minds, they had to do, and that was to deny Egypt to Africa, its natural intellectual, cultural, and physical home. Others have simply sought to minimize Egypt's contributions or to claim that to concentrate on its majesty is to miss the important point that all of Africa was not majestic. Neither was all of Europe like ancient Greece or Rome, nor was all of Asia like ancient India or China.

Listen to the ancient Greeks:

> Herodotus: "....For the Colchians are clearly Egyptians; I thought that myself before I heard it from others. As soon as it came into my head, I asked both peoples questions, and the Colchians remembered more of the Egyptians than the Egyptians did of the Colchians. The Egyptians said that they thought the Colchians were part of the army of Senusert. My own guess was based on the fact that they are black-skinned and woolly-haired; this, however, means nothing, since there are other people such. But the following is more important: that alone of mankind the Colchians, the Egyptians and the Ethiopians have circumcised from the start.

The word in the Greek text for black-skinned is *melanchroes, black-skinned.* It has the same root as *melanesia,* the black island, called such because the people there are black. Also it has the same root as the geological term *melanite,* a black garnet. The prefix "melas" means "black" and the suffix "chroes" means skin, or bark, the outer covering. The ancient Greeks said that the ancient Egyptians were *melanchroes.* But they also had *oulotriches,* "woolly hair."

Herodotus did not say the ancient Egyptians were *xanthochroes,* yellow-skinned, or *leucochroes,* white-skinned, not even *phrynechroes,* brown-skinned, but *melanchroes,* black-skinned.

Lucien relates the following dialogue between Lycinus and Timaeus:

> Lycinus: (speaking of an Egyptian boy) *This boy is not merely black, he has thick lips and legs are too thin. His hair is worn in a plait behind which shows that he is not a free man.*
> Timaeus: *But that is a sign of really distinguished birth in Egypt, Lycinus. All freeborn children plait their hair until thy reach manhood.*

Aristotle says, "Too black a hue marks the coward, as witness Egyptians and Ethiopians, and so does also too white a complexion, as you may see from women."[16]

The ancient Africans spoke of themselves as black, the very name by which they called their country, *Kemet,* "the black country" or "the black land" and *Kemetiu,* "the black people," shows that they had no problem with their physical appearance. It is important that we deal with the question of *kmt* once and for all. The word has created enormous difficulties for those who would claim Egypt for Europe. They cannot understand that the ancient Egyptians referred to their land as the Black Country and did not mean by it the black dirt or silt of the Nile. The white Egyptologists trying to make the point that *kmt* meant black land compared it to *dsrt* which they say meant "red land." But there is no exact comparison here, since the determinatives for both nouns are different. The determinative for the "red land" is the "foreign country" determinative, whereas the determinative for *kmt* is the *niwt* which means either "town," "city," or "country." Thus, *kmt* means "the Black Country."

Actually, the people who are currently called Nubians in Egypt, a black people, are the direct descendants of the ancient Egyptians. Omar El-Hakim writing in *Nubian Architec-*

*ture,* says of the Nubian architectural styles that they had been passed down to them from their forefathers, the Ancient Egyptians.[17]" In a famous painting from the walls of the tomb of Rameses III, we see another ethnology where the Egyptians painted themselves and three other nations. The Ethiopians were identical to the Egyptians in the blackness of their color, the Asiatics (as they called the Persians and Syrians) and the Libyans from the Coast were of a much lighter complexion.

Since Egypt remains the only nation of antiquity to have the physical characteristics of its people disputed by white scholars, one must ask the question, Why? The answer to this query, it seems, lies in the nature of racial supremacist theories. The early white writers of Africa's history did not have Africa at the center of their thinking; they had the superiority of whites at their center.

Comte de Gobineau and Houston Chamberlain organized a European racial hierarchy which included the Aryan, Alpine, Mediterranean types. The darker skinned Europeans of southern Europe were suspected of having black blood. In fact, Lothrop Stoddard said that Portugal's decline had resulted when they included African slavery in the southern part of the country and the blood was mixed with Africans. Stoddard popularized Gobineau's ideas.

The racist attack on Africa has been relentless even by those who have expressed knowledge of it. Henri Frankfort, historian of the ancient world, has written in an article "Myth and Reality" of the "mythopoeic thought of the Ancient Egyptians, Semites, and modern savages versus the rational thought of the Greeks and later Europeans. This notion totally disregards the mythopoeic thought in contemporary societies and the rationality of Egypt, Nubia, and other cultures of the ancient world. Euro-chauvinists and nativists claim an essentialist perspective for Europe generally, and for Greece specifically. They see it as a miracle of the white race. Barthold Niebuhr, historian of ancient Rome, stated the racist manifesto in history in these words: "race is one of the most important elements of history still remaining to be examined that which is, in truth, the very first basis upon which all history is reared and the first principle upon which it must proceed." This involved, not material circumstances or human interactions of classes and nations, but genetic endowments, racial purity, fixed and immutable national characteristics. History became to these first racial romantics the biography of race. This personification means that you can look for the origins of a race, its childhood, just like you would a human being. There was a search for the origins of the vigorous Europe. Heroic stories were published, Scotland and Germany contributed scores of folktales, but finally they would discover the European childhood in Greece. The medieval stories and the old Nordic gods and goddesses were not sufficiently heroic to go along with the new ideas of European grandeur. Wotan and Thor were no match for the ambitions of the Aryan philosophers. The Greeks would fill the bill. So in 1820, when the Greeks fought the Turks for independence, the idea of Greek origins for Europeans reached a fever pitch; indeed, the poet Shelly, could declare: "we are all Greeks, our laws, our literature, our religion, our arts all have their roots in Greece." Turkish rule over Greece was seen as an inferior race ruling over a superior one. Wilhelm von Humboldt put it this way: "...in the Greeks alone we find the ideal of that which we would like to be and produce...from the Greeks we take something more than earthly—almost Godlike." He was convinced that the Greeks represented the most perfect example of human beings, yet as a German he was captured in the context of his own ethnicity and the only way to escape the limited history of Germans was to hark back to the ancient Greeks as somehow godlike.

As descendants of such godlike beings, the Europeans considered themselves the natural rulers of the world. They then taught Africans to think of them in that way during the process of colonization. Whatever education was provided for Africans was steeped in the Eurocentric view of the world, even though the Greeks in antiquity had spoken of the things they borrowed from Egypt.

Karl Otfried Mueller, at Göttingen in the 1820's, coincidentally with the rise of Greek independence, began this new construction of antiquity. He introduced immutable characteristics of various groups to explain that Greece did not have any influences from Africa or Asia. These theories were all based on white supremacy. Furthermore, they preferred the German and English notions of freedoms rooted in the native soil to the abstract freedoms of France *liberte, egalite,* and *fraternite.* They feared the French Revolution might threaten privilege. It is the same as the Anglo-English in India, the Creole classes in many societies fearing the rise of the masses because of ideas. So they used the Greeks to serve their purposes, the purposes of the propertied classes, among other things, the slowing of democratic reform, the lack of emancipation of women, and the maintenance of a class of servants laboring for the propertied on plantations.

Thomas Macaulay showed what this social and intellectual curriculum could produce. Like Shelley or Schiller in Germany, he was convinced of the miracle of the Greeks, the divine nature and stature of the ancient Greeks. He said he "wanted to forget the accuracy of a judge in the veneration of a worshipper" when he looked at the Greeks.[18] Suppose an Afrocentrist had made such a wild statement about the ancient Africans. Macaulay could admit to having no knowledge of Arabic or Sanskrit, and yet declare in his *Minute on Education* that: "all the historical information which has been collected from all the books in the Sanskrit language is less valuable than what may be found in the most paltry abridgements used at preparatory schools in England. In every branch of physical or moral philosophy the relative position of the two nations is the same."[19]

It is not surprising that whites think in these terms, considering the information that is imparted to them on a regular basis. How else could he write? Indeed, in Macaulay's day it was clear what the purpose of the English curriculum was: "to form a class who may be interpreters between us and the millions whom we govern; a class of persons, Indian in blood and color but English in taste, in opinions, in morals, and in intellect."[20] This could be—and was—applied to Africans as well.

They stressed organicity, antiquity, pre-industrial imagery, and practiced imperialism—interesting duality of justifying imperialism in the name of conservation of a civilization which they did not create. Asia and Africa were recast as Europe's categoric inferiors. And just as our geographical regions were inferior, we ourselves were inferior psychologically and culturally. Europeans whose characters were formed with this outlook were by-and-large racists and many were asked to rule the colonial territories. They brought their attitudes to bear on the neo-European institutions that grew up with their occupation. The old traditions remained, unmoved and rooted in the structure of the people's mind, sown as it were in their blood and skin.

But the Europeans were eager to promulgate the idea of the Greeks as the masters of early human civilization. As Greeks were raised to the status of gods, Africans and Asians had to become devils.

The attack was relentless from the fifthteenth century onwards. In 1715, in the *Acta Philosophorum*, August Heumann, a climatic determinist and one of the founders of the University of Göttingen, made the distinction between Egyptian studies and Greek philosophy. There does not seem to be much difference between the two when you read the definition he gives of philosophy as the "research and study of useful truths based on reason." To imply, as he wants to do, that Africans (in this case, Egyptians) did not engage in philosophy is to assume that reason was unknown to Africa. The earliest philosophers we know—Kagemni, Merikare, Ptahhotep, Amenhotep, son of Hapu, and Amenemope—are all Africans and they lived many years before the first Greek philosopher, Thales.

J. F. Lauer amplified this racism in the twentieth century with his statement "that Egyptian priests had built up practical and technical knowledge by post facto discoveries of chance qualities that had remained totally unsuspected by their creators."[21]

For him, the Egyptians simply prepared the way for the Greeks, they were a collective John the Baptist for the real Greek messiahs. Lauer argued that the Greeks drew "from the treasure amassed by the technical positivism of the Egyptians" and thus made geometry a "genuine science."

This is an extraordinary argument, in which 5000 years of African achievement were reduced to a mere necessary backdrop to Greece. And Nubia, the mother of Egypt, is so far in the background that she fades into the night.

The racist line of thinking has been unabated. Indeed while the fifthteenth century is the great beginning of the evil influence, it seems each century since has seen its share of Eurocentric Aryanism in a self-serving way in terms of interpretation of history.

Bishop William Warburton wrote in 1730 in his book *The Divine Legation of Moses* that, while Pythagoras studied 21 years in Egypt, he did not draw his theorems until he returned to Greece. He drew the inference from this that Africans could not hypothesize, a belief that survives to this day. One might surmise, however, that he did not draw his theorems or build his schools until after he had studied in Egypt.

Since recent scholarship has shown conclusively that Egypt (Kemet) was African, now some rearguarders are trying to minimize the significance of Kemet. Thus, Mesopotamia came to the fore in their minds in the late nineteenth century, although there is nothing in Mesopotamia, Babylon, or Sumeria that equals the majesty or monumentality of the African achievement. This is not to say that An and Enlil are not important, but to place them in the same category in human history as Amen-Ra and Ptah or Atum is to turn history upside down.

Egyptian deficiencies were seen in art in Winckelmann's *History of Ancient Art* published in 1764. He argued that Egypt's art was hindered by the climate and geography not to mention the poor models, who had bandy legs and snub noses. The beautiful Greeks, on the other hand, had a good climate, were themselves beautiful, and therefore created the conditions for great art. But Winckelmann's people were to regret that he wrote what he did in 1764 before the French army entered the country. These bandy-legged and snub nosed people would be shown to be the heirs of the greatest civilization of antiquity.

He said the Greeks had noble simplicity and had serene greatness. Of course, Nietzsche and Heine were to praise the Greek and Dionysian qualities, while others praised the authoritarian and austere qualities. This was the height of propaganda.

This is a legacy of disbelief.

This is a legacy of white supremacy.

This is the legacy of white racism.

This is the limitation of Western knowledge.

In contemporary times we see that many Eurocentrists hold to these same worn-out canards and must be shown how to overcome their inner racism.

Paranoia, *para-nous*—literally—having another mind alongside one's own mind, in its original meaning in the Greek language, rather than its modern meaning of chronic delusion—describes those who have lost their own minds and who have placed another mind alongside their own. This might be the generation of paranoia.

It is important, I think, that I explain how Africa from the beginning of Europe's involvement has been strait-jacketed conceptually. It is only now that we are beginning to actually see a crack in the Western triumphalism that has plagued us for so many centuries. This has been done chiefly through language symbols and structures of knowledge. Therefore, the terms "classical," "hut," "primitive," "jungle," "tribes," and "Africa South of the Sahara" are all linked to the racist vision which limits Western knowledge. Finally, the Afrocentric vision is a human vision of balance, harmony, justice, righteousness. We are only simple human beings doing our little bit to add to the glory of human togetherness.[22]

# 4

## OUT OF AFRICA, OUT OF EUROPE: MARY LEFKOWITZ AND THE ORIGIN OF CIVILIZATION

Africa's influence on ancient Greece, the oldest European civilization, was profound and significant in art, architecture, astronomy, medicine, geometry, mathematics, law, politics, and religion. Yet there has been a furious campaign to discredit African influence and to claim a miraculous birth for Western civilization. A number of books and articles by white—and some black—conservatives seek to disprove the Egyptian influence on Greece.

One of the most recent works in this genre is a book by Wellesley professor Mary Lefkowitz, *Not Out of Africa*.[1] It continues what Martin Bernal in *Black Athena* calls the Aryanist tradition of attacking African agency in regard to Greece by raising straw-people arguments and then knocking them over.[2] This is unfortunate, but to be expected in an intellectual tradition that supports the dominant mythologies of race in the history of the West by diverting attention to marginal issues in the public domain.

Afrocentricity seeks to discover African agency in every situation. Who are we? What did we do? Where did we travel? What is our role in geometry? How do we as a people function in this or that contemporary situation? But the Afrocentrist does not advance African particularity as universal. This is its essential difference from Eurocentricity, which is advanced in the United States and other places as if the particular experience of Europeans is universal. This imposition is ethnocentric and often racist. Afrocentricity advances the view that it is possible for a pluralism of cultures to exist without hierarchy, but this demands cultural equality and respect.

Mary Lefkowitz's book has sought to re-assert the idea that Greece did not receive substantial contributions from Kemet, the original name of Egypt, which is the Greek name for the ancient land. Professor Lefkowitz has offered the public a pablum history which ignores or distorts the substantial evidence of African influence on Greece in the ancient writings of Aetius, Strabo, Plato, Homer, Herodotus, Diogenes, Plutarch, and Diodorus Siculus. A reader of Lefkowitz's book must decide if she or he is going to believe those who wrote during the ancient period or someone who writes today. History teaches us that a person is more likely to distort an event the farther away from it she happens to be. If you have a choice, go with the people who saw the ancient Egyptians and wrote about what they saw.

Conservative white columnists have felt a tremendous need to respond in the most vigorous fashion with their applause to shore up their racial mythologies. And now George Will (*Newsweek*, February 12, 1996) and Roger Kimball (*Wall Street Journal*, February 14, 1996) have seen fit to bless Professor Mary Lefkowitz's *Not Out of Africa* as a sort of definitive moment in intellectual history. It is no such moment. It is a racial argument clearly fast back-stepping. As is too often the case these days, however, Lefkowitz received the go-ahead from blacks such as Anthony Appiah and Henry Gates for her assault on Afrocentricity. It is like an African American receiving the go-ahead to attack a Jewish theory from a Jew. What this indicates is that we have gone full circle from the Hegelian "Let us forget Africa" to a late twentieth century attack on African scholarship by declaring, in the face of the evidence, that major influences on Greece were not out of Africa. And as such it will simply confirm the inability of some scholars to get beyond the imposition of the particularism of Europe. No one can remove the gifts of Europe, nor should that ever be the aim of scholarship, but Greece cannot impose itself as some universal culture that developed full-blown out of nothing, without the foundations it received from Africa.

The aim of Professor Lefkowitz is to support the unsupportable idea of a miraculous Greece and thus to enhance a white supremacist myth of the ancient world. Perhaps George Will and Roger Kimball believe that that they have found a savior of the pure white thesis. They are wrong. The thesis cannot be supported with facts although Professor Lefkowitz goes to great lengths to confuse the picture by concentrating on irrelevancies.

Mary Lefkowitz's work pales beside the research done by Cornell professor Martin Bernal in his *Black Athena*, the late Cheikh Anta Diop, in his *Civilization or Barbarism*, and former Temple professor Theophile Obenga in the important *La Philosophie Africaine de la période Pharonique*, (*African Philosophy in the Age of the Pharoahs*), or the pioneering work by California State, Long Beach Professor Maulana Karenga, *Maat, The Mora Ideal in Ancient Egypt*.

The press fanfare granted *Not Out of Africa*, however, does demonstrate how noise can be confused with music. But what is more worrisome is that it demonstrates a glee, although misinformed, on the part of those who feel some sense of relief that a white scholar has taken on the Afrocentrists, a kind of white hope idea. This stems, as I believe George Will has shown in his essay on the subject, from what is viewed as white salvation from the irrationality of Afrocentrists. It originates in an historical anti-African bias and Roger Kimball nearly gloated that readers would "savor" Lefkowitz's "definitive dissection of Afrocentrism." Contrary to any definitive dissection of Afrocentrism what Professor Lefkowitz offered was a definitive exposure of the principal assumptions of a racial structure of classical knowledge.

Professor Lefkowitz is conversant with many Greek sources but as she admits this is the first time that she has ventured into these waters. This is unfortunate because she has created a false security among those who believe that Greece sprang like a miracle unborn and untaught. Bringing Frank Snowden into the discussion of the ancient world does not help, because Professor Snowden's book *Blacks in Antiquity: Ethiopians in the Graeco-Roman Experience* is fatally flawed as a Eurocentric interpretation of the African past. His objective was to demonstrate that Africans existed in the imaginations and experience of Greece and Rome. He succeeded in stripping all agency from Africans. The problem is that Ethiopia in the form of Nubia and Kemet (Egypt) existed thousands of years before there was a Greece or Rome. To start a discussion of the ancient world at 800 B.C. E. is certainly poor scholarship. But Professor Lefkowitz's reliance on Snowden is the least of her problems.

The book is badly written and terribly redundant, as if she is in a hurry to enlarge a relatively poor argument. How many times can you really say that George G. M. James should not have used the term "stolen legacy" when he claimed that the Africans influenced the Greeks? Professor James certainly had just as much rhetorical justification as Professor Lefkowitz, who chose the unsubtle title "Not Out of Africa" probably for the same reason as Professor James called his book *Stolen Legacy*.[3]

Ruling classes always seek to promote and to maintain their ruling mythologies. Professor Lefkowitz's passion in trying to walk a tight rope between support of the false mythology of a Greek miracle and the facts of Egyptian influence on the early Greeks is telling. She seeks to minimize the role Egypt played in civilizing Greece by claiming that only in art and architecture was there real influence. This flies in the face of the ancient observers and beneficiaries of the largesse of the Africans.

Mary Lefkowitz's *Not Out of Africa* has demonstrated the tremendous power of a false idea especially, when it is advanced in the halls of the Academy. I have come to believe that it is a part of a larger falsification that encompasses the various right-wing ideologies that parade as truth. They are rooted in the same dogma: reason is the gift of the Greeks. The Greeks are Europeans, Europeans are white, white people gave the world reason and philosophy. This is not only a bad idea, it is a false idea. It is a bad idea because it preaches a European triumphalism and it is a false idea because the historical record is contrary. Tragically, the idea that Europeans have some different intellectual or scientific ability is accepted doctrine and some scholars will go to any lengths to try to uphold it. Usually, as Lefkowitz does, they commit four fundamental flaws:

## They attack insignificant or trivial issues to obscure the main points.

Professor Lefkowitz has three main axes to grind in her book. The first is that a student told her that she believed Socrates was black. The second is that the Greek gods came from Africa which she attributes to Martin Bernal, the author of *Black Athena*, and to Cheikh Anta Diop, the author of *The African Origin of Civilization*. The third is that freemasonry is the source of George James' claim in his book *Stolen Legacy* that the Greeks got many of their major ideas from the Egyptians.

The main point made by Afrocentrists is that Greece owes a substantial debt to Egypt and that Egypt was anterior to Greece and should be considered a major contributor to our current knowledge. I think I can say without a doubt that Afrocentrists do not spend time arguing that either Socrates or Cleopatra were black. I have never seen these ideas advanced by an Afrocentrist nor have I heard them discussed in any Afrocentric intellectual forums. Professor Lefkowitz provides us with a hearsay incident which she probably reports accurately, but it is not an Afrocentric argument.

I believe that both Bernal and Diop have done admirable jobs making their own cases on the legendary origins of the Greeks and I believe that readers should go to the sources themselves to see whose case, theirs or Professor Lefkowitz's, is the more plausible. I am convinced from my reading that the relationship between ancient Greece and Africa was closer and more familiar than Greece's relationship to Northern Europe.

## They will make assertion and offer their own interpretations as evidence.

Professor Lefkowitz makes a statement on page 1 of her book that "In American universities today not everyone knows what extreme Afrocentists are doing in their classrooms. Or even if they do know, they choose not to ask questions." We are off to a bad start. Who are these extreme Afrocentrists? She does not provide us with one example of something that an extreme Afrocentrist is teaching in a classroom. Not one. But already the reader is inclined to believe that something exists where nothing exists. No matter how passionate, assertion is not evidence. What Afrocentrists do teach is that you cannot begin the discussion of world history with the Greeks. Creating clouds of suspicion about scholarly colleagues in order to support a racial mythology developed over the past centuries to accompany European enslavement of Africans, imperialism, and exploitation will not dissipate the fact of Greece's debt to Africa.

**They will undermine writers they previously supported in order to maintain the fiction of a Greek miracle.**
Professor Lefkowitz and others who once considered Herodotus to be the Father of History now find fault with Herodotus because as Afrocentrists read Book Two of *The Histories,* we find that Herodotus glorifies the achievements of Egypt in relationship to Greece. In one instance Herodotus claims that the Greeks could not think that their gods actually originated in Greece.[4] But Herodotus is not the only ancient Greek writer to be dismissed by classicists who accept what Bernal rightly calls an Aryan interpretation of the ancient world.

Aristotle reported that the Egyptians gave the world the study of geometry and mathematics and the Aryanists argue that Aristotle made mistakes in what he observed. Professor Lefkowitz carries the denial of the ancient Greeks to a new level, saying essentially that you cannot trust Homer, Diogenes Laertius, Plutarch, or Strabo. Her position is that Strabo, like Herodotus, depended too much on what the Egyptian priests told him. Every Greek who wrote on the overwhelming impact of Egypt (Africa) on Greece (Europe) is discredited or set up to be discredited by the Aryanists. The idea to abandon the Greek authors rests on the belief that these ancient Greek writers cannot be counted upon to support the theories of white supremacy.

**They will announce that both sides of an issue are correct, then move to uphold only the side that supports European triumphalism**.
Professor Lefkowitz could have admitted that Egypt during the times of the Pharaohs, whatever interpretation you have of that ancient society, for example, as ornamented with Mystery Schools or simply filled with keepers of mysteries at the temples of Ipet Sut, Edfu, Kom Ombo, Philae, Esna, Abydos, and other cities, was the source of much of Greek knowledge. Rather she claims that the only real impact of Egypt on Greece was in art and architecture. This is to state

an obvious fact in order to obscure the deeper influences in science, astronomy, geometry, literature, religion, mathematics, law, government, music, medicine, and philosophy.

Not only are Professor Lefkowitz's ideas flawed, but her reasoning is faulty and cannot be sustained by any inquiry into the Greek or Egyptian languages or into ancient history. She wonders why the Afrocentric perspective is plausible to so many intelligent people. Clearly it is plausible to intelligent people because they do not believe that there was some unique brand of intelligence that struck the Greeks and created a Greek miracle willy-nilly without contact with the civilized world. In most cases knowledge builds upon knowledge. In the case of the ancient Greeks, they themselves tell us that they built upon the Egyptians. Should we believe them or should we believe the modern Aryanist interpreters who want to dismiss the ancient Greek observers?

What are the substantial arguments advanced by Afrocentrists, not the hearsay comments of a student or some rhetorical repartee between public debaters? What Afrocentrists articulate is that the Greeks were students of the Egyptians. Readers should consult the works of Yosef Ben-Jochannan and George G. M. James for themselves rather than rely on the misinterpretations and distortions of others.

On these facts we stand:

• Ancient Egyptians during the Pharaonic Period, according to ancient sources, were black-skinned Africans.

•Egyptian civilization preceded that of Greece by several thousand years.

•The great pyramids were completed (2500 BCE) long before Homer appears (800 BCE).

•Philosophy originated in Africa and the first Greek philosophers (Thales, Isocrates) studied in Egypt.

•Thales of Miletus is not a philosopher until 600 BCE.

Among Greek historians and others who wrote about what the Greeks learned from Egypt were Homer, Herodotus,

Iamblicus, Aetius, Diodorous Siculus, Diogenes Laertius, Plutarch, and Plato. Who were some of the Greek students of Africans, according to the ancient records? They were Plato, Solon, Lycurgus, Democritus, Anaxamander, Anaxagoras, Herodotus, Homer, Thales, Pythagoras, Eudoxus, and Isocrates and many others. Some of these students even wrote of their studies in Egypt as well.

There are many other points that are debatable in Lefkowitz's book, but it is not necessary to tackle each page to demonstrate that Lefkowitz has a limited understanding of the role of ancient Egypt in the foundation of European civilization as well as almost no appreciation of the fact that Egypt itself, as a gift of the Nile, was founded from the south. However, I do want to point out that she is also wrong on the issue of Alexandria. The City of Alexandria, built in honor of Alexander of Macedonia, was not a new city; the Greeks simply expanded an existing city and changed its name. The ancient Egyptian city of Rhacôtis, which probably had an even older name, was the original African city upon which Alexandria was built, much like Kinshasa under the Belgians was expanded and changed to Leopoldville. Harare under the Rhodesians became Salisbury and so forth. Triumphalism has a way of insinuating itself into everything and then claiming that it is original.

In the end I have asked myself, what is Professor Lefkowitz's point; why does she need to challenge Bernal, James, Diop, or to question my integrity? She states very clearly that her project is about sustaining the American myth of European triumphalism. In her own words:

"Any attempt to question the authenticity of ancient Greek civilization is of direct concern even to people who ordinarily have little interest in the remote past. Since the founding of this country, ancient Greece has been intimately connected with the ideals of American democracy" (Lefkowitz, *Not Out of Africa*, 1995). No one could have given a better reason than that for Professor Lefkowitz's spirited but misguided attempt to defend a falsification of history in the name of attacking Afrocentricity. When all is said and done, a more perfect union of human beings can only be based on facts.

But Mary Lefkowitz and others have often used facts within a context of white supremacist ideology. Take the attack on Martin Bernal which appeared in *Black Athena Revisited* as an indication of their fear of engaging the idea that Europe is the daughter of Africa.[5]

# THE BLACK ATHENA QUESTION

Martin Bernal has written a definitive critique of the last two hundred years of Eurocentric writings about the ancient world. The fact that he was not trained as a classicist has troubled the classicist and they have come after him with their most awesome weapons of criticism. Unfortunately, they do not have the ammunition to make a significant dent in the major interpretations of Bernal. This is not to say that other scholars do not have issues with Bernal because it is almost impossible for an objective reader not to raise questions about omissions or commissions. Nevertheless, Bernal has written an engaging and masterful work on the seizure of ancient history by Europeans. I do not believe that was his intention at all, but it has aggravated and agitated enough classicists that Afrocentrists have found the discussion and debate interesting and provocative.

It is perhaps appropriate that Mary R. Lefkowitz asks the question in the first chapter of the book, *Black Athena Revisited*, "Are Ancient Historians Racists?" The volume is edited by Mary Lefkowitz and Guy MacLean Rogers and contains chapters by eighteen authors who are pretty much convinced that few if any of the white historians of the ancient world were racists. Quite predictably Mary Lefkowitz never really answers the question she poses in the introduction and therein is the key to the book *Black Athena Revisited*.[1] The book is essentially an exercise to disprove the claims made by Martin Bernal in his monumental work, *Black Athena*, particularly volume one.

The authors of *Black Athena Revisited* are essentially agreed that Martin Bernal's *Black Athena* undercut the rather placid Eurocentric world of classicists who had been content to hide behind the enduring myth of some noble and unadulterated miracle of ancient Greece. But, alas, as Bernal discovered in his research in line with others such as Cheikh Anta Diop, Theophile Obenga, George James, and Leo Hansberry, the Greeks were but children to the Egyptians when it came to the production of knowledge in the ancient world. This is not an anti-Greek position, since all of these authors credit the Greeks with extraordinary achievements of their own.

I believe that what is especially troubling to some of the writers of this volume is that Bernal is a European scholar who, in their judgment, should have known better than to open the can of worms of racist research in the classics, a venerable taboo if there ever was one. It is a case of Bernal being viewed as a traitor to the tradition of European and American scholarship that projected the white model of intellectual development as superior to all others and consequently had appropriated so much of ancient classical Africa as a part of the "Mediterranean" or "Near East" or "Oriental" world that any breach in such a tradition had to be confronted. Mary Lefkowitz started the attack on Bernal with her book, *Not Out of Africa*. Now in *Black Athena Revisited* there is an attempt to gather additional cohorts to challenge the Afrocentrists as Lefkowitz and Rogers see it.

Nothing seems to bring out the circling of the wagons of Europe more than the questioning of European cultural superiority. Any scholar who inquires into European antiquity, particularly as that antiquity is influenced by Africa, either in terms of the first human materials or the introduction into the European societies treads on an intellectual taboo. One of the reasons Frank Snowden is highlighted and used by the classicists as an example of a black man who understands the ancient world is because his book, *Blacks in Antiquity*, is really not about blacks in antiquity but about how blacks were viewed by whites in antiquity.[2] In other words, it is a de-centered, anti-agency rendering of the African presence in the ancient world. Yet the fact remains that African civilizations, in the broad sense that the term has come to be used, antedates developments in Greece and Rome. Even classicists have now come to admit that much, as we see in several of the articles *Black Athena Revisited.* So the real question to be asked is, why have so many classicists failed to see the obvious influence of Africa on Europe, that is, particularly Egypt on Greece? If the answer is not to be found in Lefkowitz et al. (and it is not) then one must conclude that their work continues to beg the question.

Lefkowitz has a curious use of language when it comes to the role Africans played in the lives of the ancient Greeks. She argues that there were "patterns of influence," but no real borrowing of Egyptian ideas.[3] What is meant by patterns of influence? Clearly, in almost every major category of ancient life— art, architecture, ritual processions, sculpture, geometry, politics, mathematics, religion, and medicine—the Egyptians were ahead of the Greeks both in terms of absolute years and in level of sophistication during the major portion of the Greek civilization. What is more disturbing is the impossibility of Lefkowitz to admit that the ancient Africans influenced Greek civilization. To the degree that she and other classicists hold fast to such a contention, they are racist historians because their contention, in the face of evidence, is that it is impossible or improbable that a black civilization could have any significant impact on a white civilization.

And while Lefkowitz is clearly the star of this volume owing to the celebrity that came with the publication of her book, *Not Out of Africa*, she is certainly not the most combative in attacking the thesis of Bernal and the Afrocentrists. John Baines, for example, has no problem with the Eurocentric designation of Egypt as a part of the "ancient Near East" and writes "I often include Egypt under the term ancient Near East" (p. 28). The problem with Baines' classification is the same one that inflicts most classicists. They simply do not want to leave Egypt in Africa and if they do leave Egypt in Africa, they seek to take black people out of Egypt. To Baines' credit, he reviews Bernal's thesis with some accuracy, stating that the main point in the first volume of Bernal's work is that Western classicists have taken a Eurocentric view of the development of ancient Greece and that this position has often been racist in some ways.

Of course, Baines then goes on to question Bernal's emphasis on the blackness of the ancient Egyptians, saying that Bernal's treatment "seems inappropriate to any society that does not have an overriding obsession with race."[4] One could definitely argue from Baines' point of view, and indeed many have, including others in this volume; however the fact remains that a part of the intellectual glue to Bernal's thesis is the fact that so many Western scholars simply assumed that the Greek civilization owed nothing to Africa or Asia. The issue of blackness is not a major concern of Bernal's, but the issue of racism in research remained a thread in his second volume as it had been in the first. All in all, Baines' interpretation of Bernal's work is more just than some of the other authors.

Take, for example, the chapters by Frank Yurco and Frank Snowden, both rather sceptical about the ancient Egyptians being black-skinned people. They arrive at their conclusions without evidence to show that the Egyptians were other than black. In fact, there is no evidence to show that they were white or Asian. The attempt to dismiss the evidence produced by Herodotus the Greek traveler and historian who visited Egypt in the fifth Century B.C.E. demonstrates that the contemporary scholars seek to continue the Aryan Model described by Bernal. Actually, Herodotus writes very clearly in *The Histories* that the Colchians must be Egyptians because like them they are "black skinned and have wooly hair." Thus, the ancient Egyptians in the fifth century were black-skinned, not white-skinned or brown-skinned, according to Herodotus. It should be noted that Herodotus' observations came at least twenty five centuries after the founding of Memphis and therefore if the Egyptians were black when he saw them they were even blacker in the eras prior to Herodotus' visit.

Yurco, like others in the volume, spends considerable time on the race issue although Lefkowitz says in the introduction that the ancient people did not have such a preoccupation. However, it is not Yurco so much as Kathryn Bard who treads heaviest into this arena. She misunderstands the meaning of *Kmt*, so eager is she to claim that the word does not mean "Land of the Blacks." This is an issue that has been hotly debated for nearly one hundred years by European Egyptologists and Bard does not seem aware of the new line of thinking on this issue. The word *Kmt* is usually written with a hieroglyphic determinative that means *society, nation, town, place;* therefore, I have translated the term in my writings as "Black Nation" or "Black society," or literally "our society." It does not mean "black dirt" as Bard implies. The principal glyph in the word is a piece of charcoal. It is quite convenient for European scholars to find "earth" to talk about instead of the people themselves. The ancient Egyptians had black skin, whatever the meaning of that characteristic then or now; the fact remains the same. By saying this, one is not making a statement that they were Shilluk, Nubian, Zulu, Tamaschek, Yoruba, or Akan. But as these people are black, so were the ancient Kemites.

Finally, in Kathryn Bard's essay we find a discussion of the painting from Rekmire's tomb of groups of people representing different nations bringing tribute to Thutmoses III. What she fails to point out is that the Nubians and Egyptians are of the same complexion in the painting, are wearing the same clothes, and are both quite distinct from the other two representatives. Of course, we know that the Nubians and Kemites were of different nations but they were essentially of the same civilization, much like one could reasonably argue that France and Germany are different nations but of the same general civilization. Why this would be so difficult for European classicists to understand is quite beyond me. The fact that they are neighbors and of the same general African civilization does not mean either that they would not have conflicts from time to time with each other. However, what it does mean is that the Kemites did not think of themselves as a civilization widely different from Nubia. On the other hand, there are numerous references where the so-called Asiatics were thought of as quite different materially and in other ways.

What is missing in *Black Athena Revisited* is any contradiction of the principal facts advanced by Afrocentrists on the issue of African achievements, the chronological record relative to Kemet and Greece, and the extent to which African civilizations influenced Greece in areas other than art and architecture, two areas conceded by the editors of this volume.

There are some basic facts of chronology which might put the entire issue into a proper context:

• The rise of dynastic Egypt in 3100 BCE precedes even the mention of Greece by several thousand years. Homer spends seven years in Egypt and then writes the Odyssey and Iliad during the 8th century BCE.

• Imhotep, an African, is the first multidimensional personality in the history of the world and becomes the architect of the Saqqara Pyramid.

• The ninety or so major pyramids of Kemet are completed by 2500 BCE.

• Among the Greeks who claimed or were claimed to have studied in Africa were: Thales, Isocrates, Plato, Pythagoras, Anaximander, Anaxigoras, Democritus, Homer, Lycurgus, and Solon.

• Among the subjects they learned were: art, architecture, medicine, philosophy, politics and government, law, astronomy, and geometry.

Philosophy originates in Africa with the priests and their studies at the great lodges of Luxor, Abydos, Memphis, and Edfu, and the first Greek philosophers, including Thales and Isocrates, studied with the African philosophers, learning from them and disseminating what they learned in Greece.

There are far more points to be made about this volume than one could expound on in a single review essay, but I was particularly struck by the way Robert Palter tried to shore up the Aryan Model so pointedly demolished by Martin Bernal. One could almost say that Palter is so stung by Bernal's criticism of the racism of the European philosophers, Egyptologists, and historians that he leaps to tremendous heights to defend the indefensible positions of some of them. For example, we know that Immanuel Kant made racist comments about Africans. Even Palter admits as much, but then he goes on to minimize Kant's racist comments by suggesting that he did not really mean what he said because later in his life he said something different. Palter's point seems to be that if Europeans were racists, they were not such bad racists or if there were some who felt that Africans were inferior then there were others who disagreed with the majority. Or they could change their minds. He is correct on that point, as former governor George Wallace of Alabama proved that you could be racist at one point and then change your mind. I do not disagree with this, but I contend that the damage done during the period when he was pro-racist harmed the African community. The fact remains that the principal position taken by the European academic establishment of the seventeenth and eighteenth centuries was racist. This view colored their opinion of Africans in regard to the creation of the civilization of Egypt. I should point out that this was pre-eminently the period of the enslavement of Africans and the destabilization of the African continent. Egypt stands as the most remarkable example of African creation and as such it could not be allowed, by Eurocentrists, to be seen as African. If they admitted that it was African, then all of the arguments for some classical miracle of Greece go up in smoke, because how could there be a Greek civilization that did not borrow, as Herodotus claims, from the Africans?

No wonder Sarah Morris, writing the chapter "The Legacy of Black Athena," decries the concentration on Egypt in the first place. She speaks unconvincingly of a "mirage" of ancient Egypt's importance in the ancient world and sees Egypt itself as taking away from other civilizations.

Morris is way off base in primary evidence and equally as distant in terms of her criticism of Afrocentrists. There is no civilization of antiquity that she can cite which compares in grandeur, philosophy, or materiality with dynastic Egypt. To seek to marginalize Egypt, since it holds such a prominent place in Bernal's mind, as it rightly should, is to miss the mark completely. Indeed, some Afrocentrists may see her attempt to peripheralize a discussion of classical Africa as a continuation of the Aryan Model. Rather than accept ancient Egypt for what it was and has become to the world, she seems to feel a need to remove ancient Egypt as "a bone of contention" between Afrocentrists and classicists. Alas, Morris is providing too little too late; the intellectual train has already come and gone and the Afrocentrists are riding it to a re-formulation of antiquity based upon African connections and relationships that did not exist when the Aryan Model was being designed.

When Greece met Egypt in antiquity, Greece genuflected and caught the spark that Africa held and produced a light of its own. From the banks of the Nile to the sun-baked isles of Greece went mathematics, astronomy, geometry, art, architecture, medicine, and law. While *Black Athena Revisited* seeks to add to the debate surrounding Bernal's book, some of the chapters are rather acerbic and caustic in their personal tackles. This is a useful book for African scholars who are able to see in this volume all of the agency that whites give to themselves and what they take away from African Americans.

# 6

## EGYPTIAN MYSTERIES AND THE SCIENCE OF AFRICA

Among the newer claims of those who attack the Afrocentrists on the issue of ancient Egypt is that there were no such ideas as mysteries in ancient Africa. In other words, they argue that the Afrocentrists who claim that the ancient Egyptians had various secrets which their priests mastered have manufactured these mysteries. Mary Lefkowitz ties her objections to myths of the French writers of the European Renaissance, perhaps influenced by the Masonic Order, as if the French did not have access to the same information as the earlier Greeks. Indeed, the French knew quite literally, at least in the nineteenth century, and because of Champollion's breaking of the Rosetta Stone's code in order to be able to decipher the ancient Egyptian language, that the Africans had developed responses to the environment based on their own intimate ritualized knowledge and ceremonies.

Actually, the ancient Egyptians understood that all science is based on principles related to the First Time. This was not so mysterious as Westerners were later to make it, but it does provide the foundation for observational science. The First Time referred to the mythical period when the cosmic condition was defined by the gods. Everything that came after was based on the ideas established in the First Time. These principles are found first in nature and our interaction with it in a primordial way. They are not principles of the free creation of the mind; they exist in nature itself—mother, father, male, female, sky, earth, and so forth. The mind must find representation in nature, it must find its source in our history of responses. When the ancient Africans confronted this, they instituted what became known as mysteries. All societies have mysteries and the fact that the Egyptians were among the first to speak of their mysteries, to use them in ceremonies, and to initiate their priests does not lessen the reality of their investigations into the nature of being.

## GREEKS IN AFRICA

The march to Africa by Greeks began in historic times with Homer in 800 BCE. By then there were many achievements of the Africans in science, art, and literature. After Homer many Greeks came to study with the priests who were the chief scientists of the day. Going to the African continent to consult the Egyptian priests on matters of the universe, law, ethics, measurement, and astronomy became the badge of one's academic achievement.

## THE ISSUES EXPLORED

I believe that the ancient Egyptians had five questions that were important to the pursuit of knowledge:

> How to describe the indescribable?
> How to show the unshowable?
> How to express the inexpressible?
> How to seize the ungraspable?
> How to measure the immeasurable?

Here, in this construction, that is, in the answer to these questions, was the very basis of knowing. What is Medu Netcher, the sacred writing, what is African sculpture, the masks, what is music, dance, but the attempt to describe the indescribable? Is not this the very basis of what we call abstract thinking? The calendar was the basis for the structuring of the abstract concept of time. Is not the calendar among the most significant developments of human science? After all, is not time the framework for all basis in knowledge?

All African principles of knowledge, in a systematic way, rest upon the idea that before here and after, light and dark, yesterday and tomorrow, negative and positive, presence or absence, life or death, there was one incomprehensible power, unique, alone, inherent in the Nun, the indefinable cosmic sea, the infinite source of the universe outside of, that is, beyond any notion of time and space.

Every ancient center of initiation and instruction held this view. The priests-scholars of Annu (called Heliopolis), Mennefer (called Memphis), Abydos, Wenu (called Hermopolis), and Waset (called Thebes) were the keepers of the mysteries and the dispensers of knowledge to the worthy initiates.

Among the understanding that was a part of their great tradition of learning was that the greatest of all mysteries was the passage from the invisible to the visible. How do we get music from the first stirrings of the heart? What is the basis of the idea behind the historical monument? What constitutes the best way of exposing the truth and remaining in control of the knowledge of the mystery? I like to think of the mysteries like art. You draw a beautiful picture and color it, but what you are conceiving is invisible. It is only when it comes out of your brain and onto the canvas that we know it as your creation and yet this creation, was inside of you all the time. This is a great mystery.

In a modern sense it is like Wynton Marsalis hearing in his head the rhythms and melodies of twenty masters and then creating the one piece that brings all of his training and experience to life. We hear the composition and say, Wow! Man, can't he play?

Now there was something else to this idea of mystery in the ancient African mind, and that was, out of the one would come the many. From a single entity, a plurality emerged into the universe. From Ra, the Almighty, we find the creation of all the gods, humans, plants, and animals—the entire universe. But before this could be, Ra had to create consciousness in order to know that the creation of the many was possible and necessary.

## CREATION OF CONSCIOUSNESS

This originating act is sometimes symbolized by a drawn bow about to let fly its arrow. At other times it is called the *Khepera*, expressed hieroglyphically by the scarab beetle. But it is also called the stirring of Ra. One of the most important aspects of the mysteries is that Ra as the controlling force of the universe was the chief mystery maker because out of the one came the many. From one god, came the Ennead, the nine gods.

The oldest religious texts, the *Pyramid Texts*, are from tombs in the pyramid burial chambers of the 5th and 6th dynasties, long vertical columns of glyphs engraved on stone walls. These texts facilitate the king's ascension into heaven and his return to the side of his father, the supreme god. Some people think of them as magical texts or texts with magical spells and have often said that these are the real mysteries. But the pyramid texts are not the mysteries, indeed, the mysteries occurred most often in connection with the temples and not with the tombs.

In *Annu*, Atum becomes, which means that Atum must project himself or distinguish himself from the Nun. Atum sneezed out Shu, air; spat out Tefnut, moisture. Geb, earth; Nut, the sky came into being by Shu and Tefnut. Ausar, Auset, Set, and Neb-het were created by Geb and Nut. It is written that none are separate from Atum. Great Ennead is the eight plus himself which will bring order to the becoming. By self-coagulation, by his own semen, or the projection of his heart, that is, exceptional insight, Atum creates. The male seed is catalyst, a styptic fire which causes the first earth or primordial hill.

In *Memphis*, *Ptah*, creates by word; in this we can see where the concept of creation by word comes from. The Bible declares that "In the beginning was the word, and the word was with God and the word was God." But, as we know, Ra as Ptah created by the word. Creation is the ultimate end of the scientific method: to bring into existence. But how to bring into existence anything is the issue of science. There is another related issue, how to bring it in to existence with purpose, not merely for the sake of creating.

The primordial eight at Wenu were Nun and Nunet, Heh and Hehet, Kek and Keket, and Niau and Niaut. The Ogdoad, the eight, are fathers and mothers of Ra, for the child that comes forth from this primordial lotus is Ra, the principle of light itself.

> I am One that transforms into two
> I am two that transforms into four
> I am four that transforms into Eight
> after this I am ONE.
> This appears to be mystery to the ordinary person.

It is often said that *Ra* is himself the sun. That is not right, for many texts affirm that Ra penetrates the solar globe and causes it to shine, so that he renders it luminous by his passage. Ra is not light itself but that which provokes the phenomenon of light. It is found in the story of Sinuhe that the king's soul ascends to the heavens and joins with the sun disc, thus verifying the belief in the transmigration of the soul.

In *Waset*, the serpent Kamatf assimilated to Amen-Ra and the serpent Irta assimilated to Min-Amen. Also at Waset, the eight primordials, one of whom is Amen, who regenerates himself, appear as part of the division of the one. Indeed, the child is father of the present one as Ra is both child and father. To make sense of this it would seem necessary to postulate, in defiance of Western logic, that it is possible to create many from one and to have the future anterior to the past, and that a being can be his own grandfather. This is not as difficult as it seems.

One of the names of Waset is that it is the most enumerated city on earth. The great temple of Amen is said to be the place and origin and outlet of the Nun, beginning of all creative enumeration. It is the one.

I don't think the Africans sculpted the walls or wrote on papyrus with such precision only to fill them with absurdities. The work on the temples and the papyrus texts is not some joke, some comedy, it is serious philosophical thought and it is often difficult for Westerners, using a strictly materialistic mind, to understand.

Now four names of the gods are all the gods: Ra, Atum, Amen, and Ptah, who have no equal: Ra is the countenance, the Almighty; Atum is the creator; Amen is he whose name is hidden; and Ptah is the body. Even the Christian Bible says that Amen is "beginning of the creation of God" (Revelations 3:14). Their cities on earth, established in perpetuity, are Annu, Wenu, Waset, and Men-nefer.

From the moment the one regards himself there are the two opposites, and these two will take on many names. Thus, confronting order and harmony will inevitably be disorder and disharmony, a necessity inherent in creation, since nothing exists without its inverse. We see this in the activation of the texts which evoke the powers that assure order in the universe. The text says "all that has been created will return into the Nun myself alone, I persist, unknown, invisible to all." Two distinct words, *neheh* (eternity) and *djeti* (perpetuity), are double aspects of the forever. Resolution of the problems of eternity are found in the belief that the absolute being is commingled with the Nun, the infinte cosmic source of Ra, into which everything is resolved. Creation is from one into many, not from chaos into order.

Finally, this is not mysticism, not mystical but physical science; the key is lost for many of these problems and therefore they are called mysteries. Yet they are no more mysterious than when we write our names in the West in long hand and make loops for eternity as an individuation of our person. Everything ends, all begins and ends again and begins eternally.

# OUT OF HIS MOTHER S HOUSE: CRITIQUING APPIAH CRITIQUING AFROCENTRICITY

The non-white critics of Afrocentricity, often running away from their own sense of identity, tend to commit the most serious flaws in scholarship. Indeed, they are often so eager to support the Eurocentric foundation of their knowledge base that they disregard facts and run quickly to empty flourishes which have little meaning in the concrete realities of millions of African people. This is particularly true, it seems, of those of mixed parentage who are writing social justification but not history. Since there is no mixed cultural history, only national histories, these critics of Afrocentricity often are rejecting the African self to promote the European self. Inasmuch as social realities will continue to produce such individuals, we have not seen the end of the Shelby Steeles and Dinesh D'Souzas. Of course, they are not all conservative or reactionary.

One recent attempt to tackle the international Afrocentric movement is Kwame Anthony Appiah's bitter, acrimonious articles. To a large extent I believe that Appiah's own identity crisis is wrapped up in his interpretations of Afrocentricity and I have tried to deal with the particular issue of children of mixed parentage in my article "Racing to Leave the Race" in a recent issue of *The Black Scholar.* This issue is important in understanding the location of Appiah, whose companion, Henry Finder, has been an editor of *Transition* and an editor at the *The New Yorker.* Appiah is simply not speaking out of the interest of the African people, but, as is his right, out of what he sees as his individual right. On the other hand, I am writing out of a redemptionist mode because I believe that African people, of whom I feel myself most intimately a part of, have been victimized by an abnormal Eurocentrism. Appiah accepts Eurocentrism, that part of his identity that is clothed in Europe, as a mantle to be defended—even, it seems, in its opposition to Africa. This is obviously a conflictual psychological situation that speaks to either his failure to make any choice or his having chosen Europe over Africa. We are on opposite sides of the table, and while my winning does not eliminate him, his winning is meant to annihilate me. His attack on African agency is without parallel in its singular denial of the right and responsibility of African people to defend themselves on all cultural and psychological levels.

Biological dualities exist all over the place and the fact that Appiah is the product of a Ghanaian and English union does not mean that he cannot speak or should not speak of the difficulties of his own crisis. However, one must choose to speak from one place, as one can only speak from one place at a time. Appiah chooses, in his article attacking Afrocentricity, to speak and write as if he is white. Therefore my response must be directed toward one who exhibits, in my opinion, a sort of white triumphalist vision of the world. In Afrocentric theory we call it, "location." One can know where a person is located by analyzing the language that is used, how it is used, its imagery, its direction, and its mode of presentation. Appiah is clearly located on his white side. Let me hasten to add that this is not a necessary condition of biological mixtures, because there are too many scholars of mixed heritages who are Afrocentrists, such as the leading Afrocentric woman scholar, Nah Dove (*Afrikan Mothers*, 1998) whose parents were also Ghanaian and English. Of course, Nah Dove writes and speaks out of her blackness. This is not a natural location, but a choice. One makes these choices and clearly Kwame Appiah has made his choice. Much like Dinesh D'Souza's tactic of insisting that he is "colored" in order to be able to more "objectively" bash blacks, Appiah occasionally says that he speaks as a Ghanaian because his father was Asante. The Asante are a matrilineal people, however. Appiah's rhetorical claim is like Clarence Thomas saying that he speaks as a black person. In one sense it is true but in a deeper, more meaningful historical and cultural sense, one recognizes that what is considered the common economic, social, political, and intellectual interests of expanding the freedom of African people is contrary to the views of Appiah.

I believe that Marcus Garvey and Chancellor Williams were correct in their analysis of those Africans who harbored so much self-hatred that they spoke out violently against Africans who loved themselves. Just as it is sometimes important, in order to gauge objectivity, to point out whether a writer is white or black, it is also very important to know the psychological and cultural location of a writer who is assumed to be black by the public but who sees himself as neither black nor white, which definitionally, in a racist society such as the United States, is to see himself as white because in the American context you cannot be "part black" and be anything other than "black"; This situation may indicate that the person has refused to deal with his own identity in any definite terms. And if a person cannot speak out of the African cultural and historical context, then he or she should not posture *vis-à-vis* the continuing struggle for liberation; they should simply claim to be a part of the movement against Africans. All humans live in some culture, that of their fathers or that of their mothers, or somebody else's mother or father. I adamantly object to the denial of cultural place because someone is the child of an interracial or intercultural union. On the other hand, a person who claims not to be black should be questioned from the angle of his or her cultural location, since that location has historically produced an abundance of individuals who have gratuitously assaulted black consciousness; they cannot be seen to participate in cultural discussion as black. In the United States one is forced by custom and tradition, if no longer by law, to choose a cultural location because the cultures are so vastly different in their projects and in their histories, something Appiah may not be adequately aware of, since he seems much more knowledgeable of European history than he is of African American history.

Appiah establishes himself squarely in the anti-African camp while parading as an African scholar. He uses the claim of being African as a shield from behind which to attack Africans. Therefore, the Afrocentrists are not making a claim against Appiah on biological grounds but because he writes "white" in his orientations, selections, attitudes, purposes, and interests. He is misoriented because he is culturally disoriented. Thus Appiah does not attack whites who escape the burden of their brutal history *vis-à-vis* Africans, but he does attack blacks, the victims of white domination. In an article called "Race, Pluralism, and Afrocentricity," written for the *Journal of Blacks in Higher Education* (begun by a group of whites ostensibly to battle Leonard Jeffries), Appiah attacks Wole Soyinka's position because, as Appiah claims, the position "disables us because it founds our unity in gods who have not served us well in our dealings with the world" (Spring, 1998, p.116). Not only does Appiah miss Soyinka's point, he seeks to muddy the water as only he can by saying that the Afrocentrists— "like all who have chosen to root Africa's modern identity in an imaginary history—require us to see the past as the moment of wholeness and unity" (p.116). It is clear that Appiah in running away from Africa and running to Europe because it is impossible to stand nowhere; one must stand on a place, take positions, hold ground in culture or else one is in someone else's culture or pocket.

In an even more ranting article titled "Europe Upside Down: Fallacies of the New Afrocentrism" in an philosophical journal called *Sapina Journal*, Appiah argues that the Afrocentric movement is so established that it may now be called a paradigm.[1] He is correct in this observation, insofar as a paradigm suggests that an entirely new perspective on data has emerged in the scholarly literature. He is further correct to assume that it is a development that was wholly defined and projected by African intellectuals over the past two decades. However, Appiah's purpose is not to praise this new paradigm but to distort the idea. Actually, the title he uses for his article "Europe Upside Down" is revealing in itself and illustrates precisely the Afrocentrist's view of his thinking. He is unable to see Africa except in the shadow of Europe and therein is his major analytical problem, as we shall see.

In the first instance, Appiah has a problem with this Afrocentric "paradigm," because it is African or, better yet, because it is African-American-African. Indeed, he has a problem with any Africa-centered approach to knowledge, preferring what he sees as the "universal" approach to knowledge. One has only to read "white" or hear "European" where he writes or claims "universal" as an approach, since all searches for knowledge are culturally grounded. By taking the position he takes, he is only delaying the moment of Afrocentric realization if he is to continue along the path of inquiry into the nature of race and identity. It is only a matter of time in the West that one either comes to consciousness or forever buries one's head. Nevertheless, Appiah has waded into the shallowest parts of the Afrocentric ocean which, of course, is itself something of value to the unconscious. And even here Appiah is out of his depths. He claims that Afrocentricity has two basic elements, one critical (negative) and the other positive. The critical or negative thesis, he says, argues that Western scholarship is hopelessly Eurocentric. The positive thesis argues that African civilization was at the beginning of human civilization.

From this construction, an incorrect and limited construction to be sure, of the Afrocentric orientation, Appiah goes on to discuss what he sees as problematic in the construction. But he has started from a false point, an inadequate understanding of what it is he is criticizing.

The "two" elements, critical and negative, are not central components of Afrocentric theory. Appiah's attempt to put words in the text that do not have any basis in fact is cute but not the aim of any Afrocentric project that I am aware of. Indeed, he provides the worst type of anti-African logic, in a way his works speaks of self-hatred, dislocation, and the underestimating of the creative intellectual scholarship of Africans. Appiah has rarely seen an African scholar whom he respects, except perhaps a few at Harvard. He seems determined by language, attitude, and direction to distance himself from the substantive arguments made by the Afrocentrists.

My work, particularly *Kemet, Afrocentricity and Knowledge*, probably represents the worst nightmare of Anthony Appiah.[2] What is clear in that book (and my other works) is that I am confident about my sense of agency and the potential collective agency of African people long removed from a condition of agency in our own minds as well as on economic, political, and cultural terms. On a personal note, it is true that I am a student of African traditions, values, philosophies, languages, arts, and religions. Of course it is nonsense to imply, as Appiah seems to want to imply, that this means that I am antagonistic toward other cultures. In fact this reactionary tone is taken up in a line in Stephen Howe's Afrocentrism where he says that Asante's work has an anti-Arab tone. There is no evidence of this in my work nor in the work of any other serious Afrocentrists that I know. However, there are severe critiques of the way some cultures have impacted upon African people; I do not need to justify my defense of my own cultural ground.

Appiah seeks to cast his attacks on Afrocentricity in a philosophical vein, hiding behind the respectability he believes he finds in this method. But the truth will always out. He has a problem with African people viewing themselves as agents. Consequently, he seeks to turn the rightside wrong. There are several inaccuracies that he parades in his article in *Sapina* that are enough to make the journal and his attack on Afrocentricity suspect. He is either ignorant of the movement he is criticizing or a very devious writer. In either case what he has written bears little resemblance to Afrocentric theory as articulated in the many books and articles generated by either the Temple School of Afrocentricity or the Kawaida School of Afrocentricity.

Here are just a few of the inaccurate statements Appiah makes in his article:

1. *These values are often now taught in the version developed by Maulana Karenga and associated with the invention of a feast called "Kwanzaa", designed to provide an African celebration to go with Christmas and Hanukkah.*

This is a deliberate trivialization of the Kwanzaa holiday as a feast and the elevation of Christmas and Hanukkah as somehow of a different order. Is it because he has a problem with the African creation of Kwanzaa? (After all, both Christmas and Hanukkah represent human creations.) All celebrations are made by human beings. A derogatory reference to the most important African American holiday as a "feast" is an indication of the disdain that Appiah holds for African people and his inability, despite being a philosopher, to understand the concept of agency in the creative process.

2. *There is something of an irony in the use of Swahili as an Afrocentric language, since hardly any of the slaves brought to the New World can have known it.*

Afrocentricity is not a theory just for the African diaspora. In fact, Afrocentricity is fundamentally rooted on the continent of Africa, where it has its largest following. Furthermore, Swahili was not proposed as a Diasporan African language but as a language to unite Africans. It is a very logical choice and the 1977 FESTAC colloquium held in Lagos, Nigeria, concluded that it would make an excellent choice for the international African world since it was least attached to a large ethnic group such as Yoruba or Hausa. At any rate, no African slaves were brought to the Americas anyway, only African people were brought here and then enslaved. Wole Soyinka and Maulana Karenga made strong appeals at FESTAC for the incorporation of the language into the curricula of all African nations. One thing that seems lacking in Appiah's analysis is an understanding or appreciation of the historical actions of the African peoples.[3]

3. *Afrocentrists have challenged the old priority of the white Greeks by replacing them with black Egyptians.*

It is not true that Afrocentrists have replaced white Greeks with black Egyptians; we do not mind everyone standing in his or her own ground. The Greeks can remain firmly in control of whatever cultural legacy they bring the world. We simply believe that it is important to demonstrate that ancient Egyptians must be seen in the correct light. Egypt is prior to Greece as Greece is prior to Rome. We have *not* simply replaced the Greeks; we have *left* them in their place and simply unveiled the Egyptians in theirs. Historical correctness is more appropriate than political posturing.

4. *Martin Bernal is a hero of the Afrocentrists.*

To say that Martin Bernal is a hero of the Afrocentrists is inaccurate. Bernal is a very important scholar, but he is not the major voice of the Afrocentric movement. This is not to say that Bernal has not made a significant contribution to historical knowledge. But the heroes of the Afrocentric movement are numerous: Cheikh Anta Diop, Herbert Ekwe-Ekwe, Nah Dove, Ama Mazama, Chinweizu, Marimba Ani, Kariamu Welsh-Asante, Yosef Ben-Jochannan, Tony Martin, Errol Henderson, Jerome Schiele, Terry Kershaw, Miriam Maat Ka Re Monges, Katherine Bankole, Abu Abarry, James Conyers, Troy Allen, Maulana Karenga, Wade Nobles, Herbert Vilikazi, Asa Hilliard, Na'im Akbar, and scores of others.[4] And any one of these contemporary scholars could stand their ground with anyone. Bernal's work, fortunately, and without Bernal consciously intending to, supports the arguments that have been made by African scholars, and some white scholars, since the turn beginning of the twentieth century.

5. *Choosing to talk about Egypt and to ignore the rest of Africa and African history, Afrocentrism shares the European prejudice against cultures without writing.*

This is an inaccurate conclusion and it misses the point of the discussion about Nile Valley Civilizations. Egypt is to Africa in many ways as Greece is to Europe. This means that it is anterior in many concepts and constructs. To concentrate on cultures that are derived from Egypt without discussing Egypt would be like trying to shoot the rocket without fuel. If Appiah has a problem with the Afrocentric concentration on cultures with writing, then he should initiate a discussion of cultures without writing, which would be quite acceptable to Afrocentrists. Of course it is not true that "Afrocentrism shares the European prejudice" because Afrocentrists recognize language as starting on the continent of Africa. Writing is not first European; it is African first. Why should Africans not be engaged in examining all aspects of the African world? And in the end, Appiah's objections show that he is unfamiliar with the work on African oral traditions and orature by the outstanding Ghanaian Afrocentrist, Abu Abarry. Furthermore, most Afrocentrists, particularly of the Temple Circle, have studied one or more African languges.

6. *Afrocentrism persists in unanimism, the view that there is an African culture to which to appeal.*

It is true that the Temple Circle of Afrocentricity accepts the idea that Africans in Cuba, in Haiti, in Puerto Rico, in Guadaloupe, in South Africa, in Ghana, and in Nigeria respond to the same fundamental stimuli. But Appiah is wrong to speak of Afrocentrists persisting in unanimism. Most of us believe that African cultures represent different micro-responses to the environment but are similar in their broad outlines. To use the bug-a-boo "essentialism" to describe the process of self-affirmation is to mislead the reader. The term "essentialism" is often used as a term of opprobrium by Appiah and others, and the adjective "mere" has often been applied to essentialism when the critics fear any discussion of ontological bases for culture. In some ways they believe that this might endanger humanity. Essentialism should not be confused with nativism, however. Essentailism refers to the empirial fact that we are connected to our ancestors, have a certain life story, and can be identified by the stories in which we have participated. On the other hand, nativism believes that biology is the basis of a special dispensation. Appiah, being part white and part black, has found a nativistic analysis of his own with which to attack what he sees as African essentialism. What he really attacks is the right of Africans to speak as Africans because he feels that if Africans choose that right, fundamental to our existence, we then take something away from others but that is not an African way of thinking, that is precisely what we are criticizing. On the other hand, he does not attack "Scottish essentialism," "British essentialism" or "European essentialism" in any form. He has reserved his harshest criticism for Afrocentrists.

7. *Afrocentrism has ignored the writing of African scholars other than Cheikh Anta Diop.*

What Appiah means is that Afrocentrists have ignored other continental African writers, but this, too, is wrong because most of our sources *are* African. This conceptual slip shows that Appiah seeks, while sitting in an African American Studies department, to demonstrate that Africans are different from African Americans. He is trapped by false logic. There are continental Africans and diasporan Africans. Both are equally African as Jews are Jews and Chinese are Chinese and Europeans are Europeans. Show us other Africans writers who have written as Diop has written and they will become a part of our school. It is a fact that we are a particular school of scholarship and there are African writers that we refer to other than Diop but they too are Afrocentric. If we refer to Marxists like Claude Ake or Samir Amin, it is to critique them in the light of their intellectual and cultural location. If we refer to the works of philosophers such as Ogot, Houtoundji, and Appiah, it is to critique them for being off-center. V. Y. Mudimbe, whom Appiah does not mention, is a significant scholar in his own right and Afrocentrists do find much that is useful in Mudimbe (although, to be sure, Mudimbe has much to learn from the agency of Africans demonstrated in the works of the Afrocentrists). Furthermore, the African writers Chinweizu, Kofi Anyidoho, and Kwasi Yankah are just a few of the Afrocentric scholars in this school.

8. *Molefi Asante has written whole books about Akan culture without referring to the major works of such Akan philosophers as J.B. Danquah, Willie Abraham, Kwasi Wiredu, and Kwame Gyekye.*

I wish it were true that I had written whole books on Akan culture. This is certainly my ambition one day, but I am clearly a long way from that achievement. Appiah probably got me confused with some other Asante, an indication that he has not read my works. Nevertheless, Willie Abraham is one of the sources I use in my own works, particularly his book *The Mind of Africa* and I count Kwame Gyekye as a personal friend and have benefitted from his analysis. But Kwame Gyekye could have told him that I have never written a book on Akan culture. As a member of the same ethnic group as Kwame Gyekye and as the traditional Kyidomhene of Tafo, Nana Okru Asante Peasah, I would never undertake to write a book about Akan culture without the proper sources. I find it unbelievable that Appiah would make a statement about my research without examining my work or sources.

Appiah confuses Afrocentric theory with Afrocentric practice and discusses Karenga and other Afrocentric scholars in the same contexts as rap artists in an attempt to dismiss the content of Karenga's ideas. Furthermore, Appiah argues that Afrocentrists seek to give children "a diet of celebratory African history" —such as the blackness of ancient Egyptians.

I am appalled at the level of historical ignorance in which the minds of critics like Appiah are steeped. The ancient Egyptians were African and black-skinned people. The evidence for this claim is overwhelming and one has to have accepted the entire corpus of Eurocentric writing without question to dispute it. But alas, to debate Appiah on this question is rather useless, since he is not interested in the area of scholarship that would enlighten him on this subject. Let it be said, simply, that the evidence of the blackness of the ancient Egyptians has been proven by science, linguistics, history, art, and literature.

The fact that Appiah likes Clinton Jean's *Behind the Eurocentric Veils: The Search for African Realities,* a book that I read and recommended for publication because it was in the Afrocentric school, is troubling to me. It means that he clearly has no understanding of the Afrocentric project because Jean, if anything, was squarely in the Afrocentric project in the same way as other Afrocentrist theorists.[5] Prior to his death we talked and discussed the Afrocentric project and, if anything, he claimed Afrocentricity as his theoretical orientation. I wrote in support of his work because I believed in his project, which was the same project as mine. Now that I have gone through the short piece Appiah wrote for the *Sapina Journal*, let me give you my classification of African critics of Afrocentricity. There are three distinct types of such critics:

1. *Capitulationists*: These critics must condemn Afrocentricity because they are uncomfortable with themselves and do not believe that Africans should be considered agents. They believe that to project their agency is to intrude on European grounds. The operative element is self-hatred, that is, the belief that Africans are really nothing but whites in black skin.

2. *Europeanized Loyalists*: These critics are strictly into Europe; blacks can never engage in theorizing. Many Marxists and many integrationists might be seen as Europeanized loyalists. For them, any theory has to be developed by Europeans or else it does not have validity. Consequently, they never teach any black theorists, regardless of their fields of study. They are strangers to the Afrocentric idea because they have immersed themselves in only European philosophies without knowing African philosophies. They follow their own system of commandments:

> Thou shalt not accept an African origin.
> Thou shalt not mock the white man's trampling
> of other people.
> Thou shalt not threaten the cultural imperialists.
> Thou shalt not identify with any Africans.
> Thou shalt not despise the legacy of the white
> slave owner.
> Thou shalt not speak evil of Thomas Jefferson
> and George Washington.

Thou shalt not speak evil of Vladimir Lenin or
  Karl Marx.
Thou shalt not praise other African men and
  women.
Thou shalt not seek to create values for African
  survival and development.
Thou shalt not work to develop and maintain Af-
  rican identity.
Thou shalt not allow anyone to call you African
Thou shalt not quote any African theorists.

3. *Maskers*: These are the critics who are embarrassed by
Afrocentrists because we do not seem to honor whites the
same way as they do and therefore they do all they can to
conceal their identities.  Their tragedy is that they seek to
please whites by imitation, and ultmately they are disappointed
or isolated. So the maskers attack Afrocentrists to prove to
whites that they are like them. They may not harbor self-hatred but they do harbor fear.  Frightened that they may lose
their careers, they resort to vile attacks on Afrocentricity.

   In the end the entire cabal of attackers simply delays the
moment of ultimate consciousness that the Afrocentric orientation to data is not only normal but essential to African sanity.

   It is too bad that some Africans running so swiftly to support the superstructure of white racial domination have missed
their own truths. But it has always been the case that some
will not understand nor appreciate the depth of their own humanity. Africans seek no space that it is now ours and we
project no universalism that is not a combined, collective effort and project of the human race. We reject absolutely and
concretely any attempt to make of Africans anywhere little
imitations of Europe.

# AFROCENTRISM AND THE PREDICAMENT OF STEPHEN HOWE

The story is told of a hunter in the Russian steppes who went out to kill a bear who had been threatening a village. Day after day the bear would enter the village and pillage the garbage left by the villagers. Everyone was frightened of the bear because, even though he had never harmed anyone, the villagers knew that there was potential danger in the bear's visits to their community. So Ivan the Hunter decided one morning that he would go after the bear. He walked all day tracking the bear, but he could not find the terrible bear; it was as if the bear had vanished into thin air and had become invisible. Soon Ivan was tired, he had not caught the bear, and night was falling. When the night had thoroughly come over the steppes he could not see, grew frustrated, and cursed the night.

A 1998 book by Stephen Howe, *Afrocentrism: Myths* of *History*, suggests that Howe, like Ivan, has decided it is better to curse the darkness than deal with the bear. In fact, just as Ivan could not find the bear, Howe has been unable to discover Afrocentricity, and therein is his problem.

Howe says that his concern is that the Afrocentric movement has become "a cohesive, dogmatic and essentially irra-

tional ideology."[1] His concern is reminiscent of Mary
Lefkowitz's concern about the Afrocentric questioning of the
Eurocentric notion of a classical Greece untouched by Egypt.
Both are disturbed, it seems, that an intelligent, well-trained,
and committed cadre of African scholars are challenging the
central premises of white supremacy. To attack such rational
arguments against Eurocentric exclusivity in terms of knowledge, Howe resorts to name-calling, not argument, on the first
page of his book. Such a tactic prepares us for the rest of his
work, which is essentially a diatribe against what he does not
like. There is nothing wrong with one's preferences; however,
promoting one's private preferences as intellectual argument
demonstrates a limited regard for readers.

Using pejoratives to establish his orientation, Howe tries
to convince himself that Afrocentricity is a "deviation or degeneration from the wider tradition of the politics of liberation: perhaps more an index of frustration than of progress"
(p. 2). In order to buttress his orientation, Howe says that he
"tried to show that the views of writers usually labeled
Afrocentric are largely erroneous" by comparing them against
the opinions of other writers on the same themes. Of course,
what Howe succeeds in demonstrating is that he neither understands the Afrocentric idea nor can engage in sound analysis without a resort to personal attacks. Afrocentricity is not
a deviation from "a wider tradition of the politics of liberation" (which implies a European development); in fact, it is
rather the great opposition to the idea that European agency
must be cited in any instance where Africans speak in their
own voices. What Howe has attempted to do, demonstrating
his inadequate understanding of the Afrocentric project, is to
thrust Afrocentricity into some neatly packaged ideology that
he can attack as a variation, or deviation, or degeneration of
something European. Clearly, Howe is uncomfortable with
the Afrocentrists because they attack the very taboo of European superiority in civilization and culture and his only response is to argue that some will "dismiss" his ideas because

of a fixation on race to which he replies, "so be it" (p.4). Well, I would like to be the first to declare that I do not dismiss Howe's arguments because he is white; I dismiss them because they are faulty, often factually inaccurate, and based in a racist ideology of dominance.

As we shall see, Howe has written a troubling book, not so much troubling for Afrocentrists as it is for the state of Eurocentric scholarship. The book is full of innuendo, *ad hominem* attacks, false information, misleading interpretations, contradictions, and some downright careless writing about people. Alas, it is probably the best that Europe can offer as a counter to the Afrocentric philosophical inquiry and as such it is a paltry offering because it is weak, nervous, and angry. Nevertheless, it remains a useful document because it highlights the intellectual bankruptcy of those who would assault the concept of agency among Africans. In a gossipy, almost sophomoric way, Howe proceeds to take the personal lives, (for example, name changes and other details) of Afrocentric writers as his principal avenue of attack. (He does not believe for instance that my name change in 1973 had anything to do with a remark by a Ghanaian librarian to the effect that my slave-name (Howe claims that I was christened but I never was), Arthur Smith, was English. Of course, Howe could believe anything he wants to believe about why I changed my name or he could have accepted what I said, but that has little to do with the central theme of my rather extensive corpus, which obviously Howe has not read in depth nor is acquainted with if one accepts the line of argument he pursues in his book. It is one thing to scan a manuscript for tangential issues to attack and another thing to be able to grasp what a writer is saying and then be able to concretely analyze weaknesses and strengths. In Howe's world there are no strengths to the Afrocentric idea; therein is his major problem because, even if he dislikes us personally, he cannot dismiss our ideas. He pursues a negative line on every tangent he raises in his book. I am more concerned with a higher analysis of the pathetic attempt to trash the Afrocentrists and to ask the question why would the European establishment's popular presses continue to disseminate such poor works.

Howe is the poor British equivalent of Mary Lefkowitz. What she tried to do was to demonstrate that the Afrocentric idea is a threat to scholarship. Howe ends up showing that Afrocentricity is a threat, not to scholarship, but to European hegemony in science and social sciences. Indeed, it is unnecessary to question Howe's racial, ethnic, religious, or sexual background in order to demolish his arguments. Even if he were black his *ad hominem* assaults are not arguments, they are diversions from argument. What I shall demonstrate is the vacuity of the attempted arguments in his book; it is a demonstration that I can make without ever having to know anything about the man's date of birth, number of times he goes to the bathroom, or his upbringing, areas of personal life which obviously fascinate Howe.

There are three categories of arguments claimed in Howe's book, and each one can be demolished with a reading of the Afrocentric literature. In the first place, Howe lumps every African person writing favorably on Africa or African Americans as Afrocentrists. In the second place, he claims but never proves that Afrocentric scholars are creating false histories. Thirdly, he views Afrocentricity as a danger to Western Civilization.

## WHO ARE AFROCENTRISTS?

Afrocentrists tend to be well-trained scholars who are convinced that in order to understand the African world, African phenomena in the West, and African history, it is more constructive to locate oneself in a centered position and view Africans Afrocentrically, that is, from a standpoint of African agency. Of course, it is possible for individuals to claim to be Afrocentrists who are not necessarily Afrocentrists from their writings and theories. To be Afrocentric is to be quite radical because it is about a fundamental shift in the way we have viewed African people and phenomena. By presenting arguments from a different orientation and angle, the Afrocentrists have been able to shed more light on African issues than Howe cares to admit. But that is another issue with the Afrocentrists. We do not much care whether or not Howe admits something about our cultural or social history; our analyses allow us and those who are interested to have a better appreciation of phenomena that relate to African people.

It should go without saying, but obviously it must be said, that Afrocentrists have studied at the top western universities in Europe and America, but remain firmly committed to the idea that the study of Africa and Africans must be located in the interests of Africans. The rejection of a European angle on Africa is not a racist position, as Howe indicates; it is an issue of agency and centeredness. The perspectivist vision is often denied by those who want to promote the European view as universal, but that view itself is perspectivist. Howe says that many people use "mythicized self-legitimation, racially charged fantasies of origin or mystical pseudo-history," but he argues that African Americans have shown "they can be just as bad as everybody else" (p.7).

The problem with Howe is that he reveals a limited understanding of European intellectual history which should have been a prerequisite for writing about pseudo-histories and self-legitimation. If Afrocentrists have studied, analyzed, and understood anything, it is European intellectual history. After all, the education received by Afrocentrists has not been Afrocentric, but Eurocentric. It is only by virtue of self-study, not self-legitimation or mythologizing that Afrocentrists have seen the need to reject the legitimation of white supremacy. In effect, the rejection of Eurocentric hegemony is the beginning of a human possibility where the agency of Africans, Asians, and Europeans exist alongside each other. It is still possible to promote pluralism without hierarchy as the Afrocentrists have always claimed.

## WHAT ARE THE FALSE HISTORIES ANYWAY?

Historians of one epoch, of one ethnic group, and of one persuasion will tend to create history as self-confirmation unless checked by the restraint of logic, review, and peer evaluation. Howe is careful not to cite the many cases where Afrocentrists have highlighted the way European historians have twisted the truth. Rather he claims that the Afrocentrists, the correctionists, are the ones who are promoting false histories without examining in any depth the major thesis of Hegel, the dominant historical philosopher of the European civilization.

This is not the place to give Howe a lesson in history, but I believe that anyone writing about false histories must have some understanding about the nature and role of history itself, otherwise the tyrannies of environment and politics and racism continue to reign over all discussions of histories. All history is selective. No one writes a complete history of any human society, and to the degree that Howe believes that Europeans have done so—or at least, to the degree that he sees Afrocentrists as writing false histories and Europeans as not writing false histories—just to that degree has he beguiled himself.

What Afrocentrists have done during the Afrocentric Revolution is to challenge the limited perspective of Europe by engaging in the correction of an overbearing emphasis on the European Age, the Greek Miracle, the European Century, the Enlightenment, or any other sort of white triumphalist vision of the world. But this challenge can be considered "false histories" only by those who would take all history as reflective of only Europeans and their agency. It is the Afrocentrists wish that, by making Europeans more conscious of their pedestrian provincialism parading as universalism, they will be enable Europeans to transcend their own biases.

All history is selective; one never includes all the facts in any historical account. Howe may not like the reality that Afrocentrists have chosen to select from a multiplicity of facts and sequences of causes and effects those which are of historical significance to Africa rather than to Europe, but he cannot change the reality that Africa is not Europe. What he may claim as significant from a European conceptualization may be irrelevant to the pattern of argument that the Afrocentrists advance. That is why Afrocentrists have argued that we do not seek to impose our worldview on others; we seek only to demonstrate that our model of analysis has a far greater explanatory power in terms of our own agency. Contrary to Howe's fear, this is neither mysticism nor cynicism; it is Afrocentric realism.

Given that Howe has written of me as the "Godfather of Afrocentrism" (with all of the connotations that term conjures), I suspect he believes that by attacking me he gets at the core of "Afrocentrism." This is a mistake, and he knows it; that is why in the very next chapter in his book he writes of "The Network, the School and the Fellow-Travellers." I want to particularly take issue with his attempt to categorize my own work and the numerous erroneous statements he makes, some of them made by him, but appearing to be made by me. For example, he writes, quoting me, "Ebonics the language spoken in the United States by African Americans which uses many English Words but is based on African Syntactic elements and sense modalities."[2] Then he adds, "These are superior to those of other groups, and especially to those of European-descended peoples."[3] Of course there is nothing like the latter sentence in any of my works and Howe's gratuitous addition of it appears devious. There is nothing in my scholarship that speaks to superiority. Of course, I may have spoken at times of what is more grounded in the African American culture as being more comfortable, consistent, and persistent in our history as a cultural form, much like one would speak of a yokel yodeling in Howe's culture, perhaps, as being more consistent and more persistent in the people's history. But there is never a hint of superiority in my own writings.

But Howe's intellectual deviousness and nastiness do not stop with tagging sentences; they extend to speculations that have nothing to do with scholarship or with fact. For example, in one section he writes that "Van Sertima is more cautious and coherent in his procedures than most Afrocentric writers (and is clearly disapproved of by many of them)."[4] In a note, Howe continues (about Van Sertima), "he and his disciples' writings are rather conspicuous by their absence from the bibliographies or acknowledgments of Molefi Asante and the Temple Circle, as well as those of Karenga, Carruthers, and their circle—and vice versa."[5] Howe shows his duplicitous nature with this discussion. He has already dismissed the research of Ivan Van Sertima, suggesting that "Van Sertima's grab-bag of evidence for such culture contact amounts mainly to a superficial and highly selective list of alleged similarities between Egyptian and Meso-American cosmologies, architecture, and so on" and furthermore "the generally rational approach was, however, confused or undermined in *They Came Before Columbus* by the dramatizing even fictionalized, narrative style."[6] This schizoid sort of writing characterizes so much of Howe's book that it can hardly be taken seriously. He would have done much better simply concentrating on one or two authors and doing an extensive and intensive interpretation of those works. On Van Sertima, as on other African American writers (and Van Sertima has never declared himself an Afrocentrist), Howe does not know whether to indict, acquit, convict, or admire. Yet he castigates Afrocentrists for not citing Van Sertima and, of course, says Van Sertima does not cite Afrocentrists. This is pettiness at its worst and can only be viewed as Howe's attempt to stir up trouble where there is none. Most scholars stick with what they know and use the sources that support their ideas and arguments. I believe had Maulana Karenga, Kariamu Welsh Asante, or Marimba Ani found a reason to cite Van Sertima they would have, and vice versa. As for me, I have never declared knowledge of the Meso-American area and have every respect for the role Van Sertima and others have played in demonstrating the African presence in that part of the world prior to colonization by the Europeans. At any rate, *Introduction to Black Studies* by Karenga cites Van Sertima extensively.

## WHY IS AFROCENTRICITY DANGEROUS?

Samir Amin wrote in *Eurocentrism* that the one great taboo violated by the radical writer was to question the European ideal itself. Nothing is radical if it does not seek to alter the basis upon which racism, sexism, classism, and poverty are based.[7] Afrocentrcity is considered dangerous because it indicts gross Eurocentrism as racist, sexist, classist, and homophobic. It is considered dangerous because the Afrocentrist finds the impressive data collected by various scholars on the origins of civilization in Europe useful and refuses to dispense with the information simply because conservative white scholars do not find the data in agreement with the orthodox and received version of European history. This is not to say that everything in the works of Gerald Massey, David MacRitchie, Ahmed and Ibrahim Ali is accurate; however, their views are just as well argued as those of other writers. The fact that they have not gained the ascendancy in intellectual traditions in Europe has as much to do with the accepted line of thinking as with their evidence. Howe dismisses them as he tries to dismiss Afrocentrists because he apparently has some investment in the idea of a Europe without African influence.

There is not one instance where Stephen Howe has proved that Afrocentrists have argued a false history. In cases where there are speculations on ancient migrations, such as the Olmec civilization in Meso-America, the evidence given by the Afrocentrists is as valid and plausible as that given by other scholars. Speculation, based on the best available evidence, within the framework of a historical argument, guides most scientific analysis; the same is true for Afrocentricity.

# 9

# ERICH MARTEL AND THE
# FALSIFICATION OF ANCIENT AFRICA

Ancient Egypt has become one of the most contested arenas in the present social studies curriculum in American public schools, largely because it is located on the African continent. Of all of the ancient civilizations, only ancient Egypt has evoked an argument about the ethnicity of its ancient people. No one questions whether or not the Chinese were really Indians or the Greeks were really Mongolians. Erich Martel, a Washington, D. C., high school teacher, and Frank Yurco, a graduate student at the University of Chicago, have become regular critics of the way ancient Egypt is beginning to be taught in many schools. They tend to see danger in three areas: (1) the loss of Eurocentric control over the substance of Ancient Egyptian history, (2) the Afrocentric critique of the racism of nineteenth and twentieth century Egyptologists, and (3) the attack on the claim by Eurocentrists that the ancient Egyptians were whites.

Of course, there is a subtext to this position that goes back to 1798, when the French invaded Egypt. This invasion, the first major invasion of Egypt by a European nation since that of the Greeks in the Fourth Century B.C.E. was accompanied by writers and artists under the direction of Dominique Vivant Denon. They had as their objective the recording of everything they could discover in Egypt. So artists gave their renditions of temples, tombs, wall paintings, and other works from Egypt. Writers described as best they could the massive works they saw in the Nile Valley. A book, *The Description of Egypt*, was published and created a stir in Europe because it brought to the attention of European academics in stunning fashion the immense contributions which civilizations in Africa had made to the world. But how could this be, since for three hundred years Europeans had taught themselves and anyone who would listen that Africa had produced nothing and was, as Hegel would say, no part of human history?

To maintain in the face of the most monumental ancient civilization on earth the fiction that Africa had created nothing, European writers had to define Egypt out of Africa. The idea was that Egypt was not African. To further support this line of thinking, Egypt had to be divorced from the nations and peoples who were contiguous with that ancient land. After Champollion had deciphered the hieroglyphics, the aim was to translate words as Eurocentrically as possible. Thus, the word "NHSI" becomes Negro even though the usage of the term is national rather than racial. Similarly, the word "KMT" is translated "The Black Land" when it really should have been called the Black Country. All of these stratagems were used to take Egypt out of Africa. Unfortunately, we still have latter-day would-be egyptologists trying to perpetuate the same kind of "sever Egypt" philosophy.

The truth of the matter is rather simple for teachers. Egypt is on the continent of Africa and the ancient Egyptians were black-skinned people, meaning they were Africans. When one speaks of ancient Egypt one is usually talking about a period from 3100 B.C.E. to around 333 B.C.E. This period of Egyptian history was made by black-skinned people. Several invasions—Persian, Assyrian, and Greek—took place between these dates. However, the character of Egypt remained African and its people remained black-skinned without much intermixture until the coming of the Arabs in 639 C.E.. Teachers must be clear in their understanding that the Arabs are not indigenous to Egypt. They must understand that Arabic is not an African language and is certainly not the language spoken by the ancient Egyptians. They spoke an African language, Egyptian. This is the language whose "hieroglyphic" script is ubiquitous on the walls of the pyramids and temples of Ancient Egypt. Therefore, when someone attempts to paint ancient Egypt as a multiracial enterprise, they are giving misinformation. It is only done as a hold-over from the racist science of the early Egyptologists who, while admitting that it was true as Aristotle and Herodotus said that the ancient Egyptians had black skin and wooly hair, claimed that they were "black-skinned" whites! Such blatant disregard for facts and the records of Europe's own early scholars leads to artificial defenses of the status quo and a white racist rendering of an ancient African civilization in most of the contemporary text books. The fact that this racist rendering is "received" from the early egyptologists, most of whom were themselves racist (as shown by Miriam Monges in *Kush: The Jewel of Nubia*), has little to do with what ought to be taught.[1]

On the question of race, the teacher must teach the truth as it is revealed in the writings and paintings of the ancients themselves. They were black-skinned people. They were not confused over this issue, and in the first exercises in ethnology in human history, they painted themselves and the ancient Ethiopians as black, while two other races were shown as pale.

There are some overarching approaches to the teaching of Egypt that are important for an accurate portrayal of ancient Africa:

1. *As a fundamental principle, use textbooks and supplements that display authentic, primary-source depictions rather than a modern artist's rendering or illustration.*

In order to support the notion of ancient Egypt as a white civilization, it was necessary to avoid the use of any authentic Egyptian paintings unless, of course, they are the paintings from the period of Greek occupation, the Ptolemaic Dynasty. There had been more than thirty dynasties in Egypt before the Greeks conquered the government in 333 B.C. Thus, when a teacher or a writer such as Erich Martel talks about the ancient Egyptians being white, he must be questioned as to which time period is he referring to. There are no indications in history of ancient Egyptians being anything other than Africans, blacks, unless one refers to the conquerors or invaders who came into the land. The use of authentic paintings and documents from Egypt will provide students with a better representation than illustrations filtered through a modern artist's eyes.

2. *Teachers should call people and their lands by the same name as the people themselves did do.*

Thus, ancient Egypt was called "Kemet" by the ancient people of that civilization. A teacher certainly can indicate that "Egypt" is a Greek word and was not used by the "Egyptian" Africans with reference to themselves in ancient times. The ancient people of Kemet also called themselves "Kemetcu," which means "the black people." At other times they referred to themselves simply as "Remetchu," the humans. Afrocentrists also claim that the use of pejoratives such as "Bushmen," "pygmy," and "Hottentot" serve to minimize the agency of African people. No Africans call themselves by those names. Similarly, in the context of ancient Africa, we should call the people what they called themselves.

3. *Teachers should relate ancient Egypt to ancient Nubia and other civilizations along the Nile.*

A favorite activity of some teachers is to relate the classical civilizations of Africa to European or Asian civilizations without the slightest thought that they are more sensibly related to the other African civilizations on the same continent. Egypt/ Kemet, for example, has more in common with Nubia than it does with civilizations across the Mediterranean, yet one would hardly know this by referring to most texts on the subject. Egypt relates to other African nations in almost every respect in architecture, governance, totemism, ancestralism, agriculture, writing, music, and theology. This is the obvious connection and the one that is avoided by most teachers who follow the Erich Martel model of minimizing the importance of Egypt as a culminating civilization of the ancient African people.

# 10

## CONCLUSIONS: A RESTATEMENT OF AFROCENTRIC SYSTEMATICS

I offer this short chapter as a contribution towards clarifying the issue of Afrocentricity. In commentaries, one by Henry Louis Gates, Jr. on a Washington radio program, and another by the white writer Sidney Mintz, I have noticed confusion around the theory of Afrocentricity. I certainly would not claim that such ambiguous discussions of the idea are deliberate; they are nevertheless misleading and should be corrected. Gates, for his part, admitted that "all of us in African American Studies are Afrocentrists," a questionable statement in itself; however, he continued that there were certain Afrocentrists with which he did not identify. That would be fair enough if he had defined what he meant by Afrocentricity in the first place. Rather than engage the idea as I have explained it in several books, Gates attacks straw-men arguments that have not been made by any Afrocentrists. Mintz, on the other hand, in advancing his theory of our culture, attacks Afrocentrists in the *Chronicle of Higher Education* as disagreeing with something that we—at least, I—had never read. Both of these remarks suggest gratuitous commentary about the growing Afrocentric school of thought. There have been other such statements expressed, mainly in press releases, public relations brochures, and interviews in the white media. Most of the comments proceed from ignorance of the concept.

One could easily say that he or she does not identify with this or that deconstructionist, but in the minds of Gates and Mintz there is something that is not quite right about the world view of the Afrocentrists. Indeed, it may be the term itself. They see in the term "Afrocentricity" the idea of Africans taking the role of Europeans, that is, African experience as the only universal one. But this has not been the direction of afrocentric theory or philosophy. It has been clearly articulated in scores of articles and books. What is at stake, however, is the interpretation of the African's role in the future. The Afrocentrists have opted for agency. This has created a dichotomous situation where there are those who seek agency and those who see addition. The adders are those who simply want to be added to the Eurocentric world or to have the Eurocentric view open up to them. The Afrocentrists, on the other hand, believe strongly in the autonomy of the African agency, even an autonomy that gives the African the right to choose or not to choose to ally at certain points. In analysis, this means that the Afrocentrist seeks any method to explicate the agency of Africans in any given situation.

Since my works (*Afrocentricity*, 1980; *The Afrocentric Idea*, 1987; and *Kemet, Afrocentricity and Knowledge*, 1990) constitute the major corpus in the Afrocentric movement, I have accepted the challenge suggested by my colleagues to write on the systematics of Afrocentric theory in response to some of the commentaries. I had hoped that the numerous publications in this emerging tradition would have been engaging enough, but it appears in many cases that those who have commented upon Afrocentricity have not read the literature and have therefore reacted to the concept much like Europe reacted to Africa for nearly five hundred years—that is, try to control it, trivialize it, or destroy it, but never study or learn from it. Gerald Early's "Understanding Afrocentrism: Why Blacks Dream of a World Without Whites," published in the journal *Civilization,* is a case in point.[1] Early writes a terrible essay, full of Wodenic magic, misinformation, and obscene catering to white triumphalist sentiments. He argues that Afrocentrism, a misnomer, is issues such as the blackness of Jesus, the Mario Van Peebles movie *Posse,* Kwanzaa, and a religious orthodoxy. While he does claim that it is an intellectual movement, he moves quickly to emphasize what he sees as the political and religious nature of Afrocentricity. For the confused Early, even Louis Farrakhan is an Afrocentrist. Indeed, any African person who speaks in the interest of African Americans might be considered an Afrocentrist under his characterizations. By claiming that Farrakhan is probably "the most familiar figure associated with Afrocentrism," Early positions his argument in an anti-African, anti-Islamic mode. It is anti-African because in attacking Farrakhan as a political leader, he is distorting the role of Afrocentricity as an intellectual theory for analyzing African behavior. It is anti-Islamic because he raises the issue of Farrakhan's speech with a "militant flair and a racist edge" as a sort of gratuity to his white readers. Like his previous attacks on Malcolm X, Early seeks to damage the image of Farrakhan as an icon of the black community. He re-hashes the allegations of Farrakhan's attacks on Jews. He claims that "Afrocentrism" rejects cosmopolitanism as being white or Eurocentric without giving one instance where that is so. Early does not know that George G. M. James was a college professor and dismisses his book without having discussed it in any detail—an obvious indication that he has not read it. Similarly, he dismisses Tony Martin's important book, *The Jewish Onslaught: Despatches from the Wellesley Battlefront,* and claims that the book *The Secret Relationship Between Blacks and Jews* is anti-Semitic without showing one sentence or quote to back up such a preposterous claim.[2] Gerald Early's essay is pieced together from the same conservative information packet that was sent to thousands of newspaper offices and schools during the time that Arthur Schlesinger's book, *The Disuniting of America*, was being freely distributed by Whittle Communications. What seems to unite these responses to Afrocentricity is the generally inadequate analysis of the theoretical position that has been taken by the scholars in this field.

The often flippant responses to Afrocentricity have underscored the point usually made by Afrocentric scholars, namely, that the imposition of the Eurocentric perspective on every subject and theme as if the Eurocentric position is the only human and universal view is the fundamental basis of a racist response to history. That it has affected and infected the Academy should come as no suprise since it was in the same Academy that the ideas of white supremacy were propounded for centuries in Germany, France, England, and the United States by the likes of Hegel, Voltaire, Toynbee, and others. If anything, our contemporary universities are the inheritors of this vicious virus that erodes the very nature of our seeing, our explanations, our methods of inquiry, and our conclusions. Sidney Mintz's conclusion about what Afrocentrists would agree with or not agree with in his article "The Birth of Afro-American Culture" is just such an example. He demonstrates no knowledge of the Afrocentric position on the question of the origin of African American culture. I can almost guarantee, however, that if his essay on Afro-American cultural origins does not proceed from an African American perspective he will be highly criticized by Afrocentrists. To study African Americans as side-shows to whites, as marginal to history, as detached from place and purpose is to study amiss.

Afrocentricity is primarily an orientation to data. There are certainly data and facts which may be used by Afrocentrists in making analyses, but the principal component of the theoretical piece has to do with an orientation, a location, a position. Thus, I have explained in several books and articles that

Afrocentricity is "a perspective which allows Africans to be subjects of historical experiences" rather than objects on the fringes of Europe. This means that the Afrocentrist is concerned with discovering in every case the centered place of the African. Of course, such a philosophical stance is not necessary for other disciplines; it is, however, the fundamental basis for African or African American Studies. Otherwise, it seems to me that what is being done in African American Studies at some institutions might successfully be challenged as duplicating in content, theory, and method the essentially Eurocentric enterprises that are undertaken in the traditional departments.

African American Studies, however, is not simply the study and teaching about African people but it is the Afrocentric study of African phenomena; otherwise we would have had African American Studies for a hundred years. But what existed before was not African American Studies but rather Eurocentric study of Africans and other "Third World" peoples. Some of these studies led to important findings and have been useful. So the Afrocentrists do not claim that historians, sociologists, literary critics, philosophers, communicationists, and others do not make valuable contributions. Our claim is that by using a Eurocentric approach they often ignore an important interpretative key to the African experience in America and elsewhere.

This, it seems to me, poses a special problem to those who teach in African American Studies because the field is not merely an aggregation of courses on African American history and literature. Without a fundamental orientation to the data that centers on African people as subjects and agents of historical experiences, the African American Studies programs are nothing more than extensions of the English, history, or sociology departments. On the other hand, the Afrocentric study of phenomena asks questions about location, place, orientation, and perspective. This means that the data could come from any field or place and be examined

Afrocentrically. At Temple University we experiment with materials as varied as literary texts, architectural designs, dance aesthetics, social institutions, and management techniques to teach the concept of centeredness.

Like scholars in other disciplines, Afrocentrists are exposed to the hazards of place and position. We can never be sure that our place is as secure as we want it to be, but we do the best we can with the resources of mind at our disposal. The aim is to open fields of inquiry and to expand human dialogue around questions of social, economic, historical, and cultural concern. Everything must be run through the sieve of doubt until one hits the bedrock of truth. Our methods, based on the idea of African agency, are meant to establish a clear pattern of discourse that may be followed by others.

Afrocentricity is not a matter of color but of perspective, that is, orientation to facts. The historian, sociologist, psychologist, and political scientist may examine the Battle of Gettysburg and see different elements and aspects because of the different emphases of the disciplines. In a similar manner, the Afrocentrist would look at the Civil War or any phenomenon involving African people and raise different questions than the Eurocentrist. These questions are not more or less correct, but better in an interpretative sense if the person doing the asking wants to understand the phenomena in a given context. Since the Afrocentric perspective is not a racial perspective but an orientation to data, anyone willing to submit to the rigid discipline of the field might become an Afrocentrist. This is why there are a growing number of Chinese, Dutch, German, and Japanese scholars who have taken up the study of Africa and African America from the standpoint of Afrocentricity. They are Afrocentrists.

There are two general fields in which the Afrocentrist works: cultural/aesthetic and social/behavioral. This means that the person who declares in an intellectual sense to be an Afrocentrist commits traditional discipline suicide because you cannot, to be consistent, remain a traditional Eurocentric intellectual and an Afrocentrist. Of course, there are those who might be bi-positional or multi-positional under given circumstances. In claiming this posture, I am not dismissing the work that has been done in other fields on Africans and African Americans; some of it has enlarged our understanding, particularly that work that might be considered pre-Afrocentric, such as the works of Melville Herskovits, Basil Davidson, Robert Farris Thompson, and other scholars who have sought to see through the eyes of Africans and to place Africans in a subject rather than object position.

Afrocentric theories are not about cultural separatism or racial chauvinism. Among those who have been quoted as making such a charge are Michele Wallace, Arthur Schlesinger, Miriam Lichtheim, Cornel West, Diane Ravitch, bell hooks, and Henry Louis Gates, Jr. With such an unlikely crew in the same bed one is eager to discover the source of their offhanded remarks about Afrocentricity and separatism or chauvinism. Attempting to give them the benefit of the doubt, I have assumed that they sense in the Afrocentric perspective a pro-African and an anti-White posture. Apart from the fact that one can be pro-African and not anti-White, the concept of Afrocentricity has little to do with pros and cons; it is preeminently about how you view phenomena. Of course, I have always been unashamedly and unapologetically African. But this is no reason to condemn or dismiss the theory of Afrocentricity.

I believe that the white scholars who register a negative reaction to Afrocentricity do so out of fear. The fear is revealed on two levels. In the first place, Afrocentricity provides them with no grounds for authority unless they become students of Africans. This produces an existential fear: African scholars might have something to teach whites. The Afrocentric school of thought is the first contemporary intellectual movement initiated by African American scholars that has currency on a broad scale for renewal and renaissance. It did not emerge inside the traditional white academic bastions.

The second fear is not so much an existential one; it is rather a fear of the implications of the Afrocentric critique of Eurocentrism as an ethnocentric view posing as a universal view. Thus, we have opened the discussion of everything from race theory, ancient civilizations, African and European personalities, the impact of the glaciers on human behavior, and dislocation in the writing of African American authors. We examine these topics with the eye of African people as subjects of historical experiences. This is not the only human view. If anything, Afrocentrists have always said that our perspective on data is only one among many, and consequently the viewpoint, if you will, seeks no advantage, no self-aggrandizement, and no hegemony. The same cannot be said of Eurocentrism.

The African American and African Eurocentrists are a special problem. They represent two cases. The first case is represented by those who have been so well-trained in the Eurocentric perspective that they see themselves as copies of Europeans. These are the Africans who believe they came to America on the *Mayflower* or, better yet, that classical European music is the only real classical music in the world. Their rejection of Afrocentricity is tied to their rejection of themselves. Thus, the inability to see from their own centers or to position their sights on phenomena from their own historical and cultural conditions is related to what Malcolm X used to call "the slave mentality," that is, the belief that their own views can never be divorced from the slave-master's. To a large degree these Africans tend to lack historical consciousness and find their own source of intellectual satisfaction in the approval of whites, not in the search for the interpretative key to their own history. I am not suggesting the stifling of this type of imitation in any politically correct way, but rather I want to explain the response to Afrocentricity in an historical manner. The second case is also historical, that is, Afrocentrists find evidences of it in our historical experiences. These are the Africans who seek to be appointed overseers on the plantation. They do not necessarily believe they are the same as whites. They recognize that they did not come here on the *Mayflower,* but they aspire to universalism without references to particular experiences. For them, any emphasis on particular perspectives and experiences suggest separatism and separatism suggests hostility. This is a fallacy because neither separatism nor difference suggests hostility except in the minds of those who fear.

In an intellectual sense, these African Eurocentrists feel inclined to disagree with any idea that has popular approval among the African American masses. Much like the overseers during the ante-bellum period, they are eager to demonstrate that they are not a part of the rebellion and that they discredit the ideas that are derived from the African masses. They might even consider themselves a part of the elite, almost white, separate from the rest of us. The progression of their *clarencization* is seen in the distance they seek to place between themselves and us. Indeed, they might even participate in what Louis Lomax once called "the fooling of white people" by telling white audiences that Afrocentrists represent a new and passing fad.

The point is that Afrocentricity is nothing more than what is congruent to the interpretative life of the African person. Why should an African American see himself or herself through the perspective of a Chinese or white American? Neither the Chinese nor the white American views phenomena from the perspective of the African American; nor should they. Historical and cultural experiences and traditions differ, and in order to understand the African American experience in dance, architecture, social work, art, science, psychology, or communication, one has to avail one self of the richly textured standing-place of African Americans. In the end, you must ask yourself, Why does such a simple rational position threaten so many people?

# Notes

## Preface

1. Maulana Karenga. *Selections from the Husia: Sacred Wisdom of Ancient Egypt.* (Los Angeles: University of Sankore Press, 1984.) This was the first translation of the ancient wisdom of Egypt by an Afrocentric scholar.

2. The book *Eurocentrism* (New York: Monthly Review Press, 1987) by Samir Amin was one of the first examples of locational theory being applied to Europe itself. The idea in Amin's work is that the taboo of discussing Europe alongside other civilizations had to be broken and then we could speak of a more harmonious world. Despite the values found in European documents it was difficult to find such values repeated in the history of the people. Other cultures may not have had the values spelled out but they operated in more humane ways. Some societies without writing have demonstrated that personal and communal relationship was more significant for them than individualism.

3. There is a considerable amount of information written about the distinctions between Eurocentrism and Afrocentricity. Indeed, in my book *Kemet, Afrocentricity and Knowledge* (Trenton: Africa World Press, 1990) I dealt with this issue. Others, such as C. T. Keto, *An Africa-Centered Perspective of History* (Blackwood, N. J. 1991, discussed the issue of hegemonic Eurocentrism, as opposed to ordinary Eurocentrism which everyone pretty much believes is normal.One expects people of European heritage to respond to motifs and examples that come out of that cultural experience.

4. The article by Kwame Appiah, "Race, Pluralism, and Afrocentricity," in *Journal of Blacks in Higher Education*, (Spring, 1998): 116, is an

example of a writer with a partly African heritage defending Eurocentrism. While Appiah's defense of the indefensible seems unjustified, I believe that it is perfectly logical within the context of his own personal quest for identity.

5. Leonard Jeffries, "RA-demption and the African American Community," lecture delivered at the Temple of Africa, Philadelphia, November 14, 1998.

6. Cheikh Anta Diop, the late Senegalese scholar, wrote *The African Origin of Civilization* as a primer to the debate over the ethnicity, indeed, the color of the ancient Egyptians. Additionally he was the author of *L'Afrique Noire precoloniale; Nations negres et Culture*; and *L'Antiquite africaine par l'image.* Although his corpus has not yet been adequately assessed by Afrocentrists, he is, based upon the previous locations of his work, undoubtedly the most significant Afrocentric precursor.

7. Diop's book *The Cultural Unity of Black Africa* (Paris: Presence Africaine, 1959) became a major handbook for Pan- Africanists and cultural thinkers interested in seeing a United States of Africa.

8. Chris Gray, *Conceptions of History: Cheikh Anta Diop and Theophile Obenga* (Chicago: Karnak House, 1994).

9. See Theophile Obenga, *African Philosophy in World History*, (Princeton: Sungai, 1998), p. 12.

10. See Chukwunyere Kamalu's *Foundation of African Thought*, (Chicago: Karnak House, 1995).

11. See C. T. Keto, *Africa-Centered Perspective of History* (Blackwood, N. J.: B and K, 1991) and Linda James Myers, *Understanding the Afrocentric Worldview.*

## CHAPTER ONE

1. This is not just a long list of African and African American writers and scholars; this is a refined list of some of the most thoughtful social, historical, and philosophical thinkers of the nineteenth and twentieth centuries. Their works appear in a host of journals and books.

2. Afrocentricity did not arise as a political idea but a philosophical or theoretical position. One may use it politically as one could use existentialism or Marxism politically, but the individuals named in this section are people who have declared one way or the other that to study African phenomena you must view Africans as agents, not as servants, subservient, or fringe people. Centering the subject rather than objectifying the study of Africa is indeed quite a discipline and few have been able to master it.

3. These two books were written during a particularly fruitful period in Buffalo, New York when the Center for Positive Thought was in the process of expanding its services to include the arts and antiquities of Africa and Africa America. *Textured Women, Cowrie Shells, Cowbells and Beetlesticks* became the first truly self-conscious Afrocentric poetry book. It was published by Amulefi Publishing Company in 1979. It broke with the Black Arts Tradition by claiming Afrocentricity as the core of the artistic project. No longer was the writing just *about* Africans, but it *was* Africans speaking, acting, and doing. It is true, however, that Larry Neal and Maulana Karenga had called for a black frame of reference during the Kawaida inspired Black Arts Movement.

4. See chapter on Stephen Howe's *Afrocentrism* in this volume. I debated Stephen Howe on the British Broadcasting Company in the Fall of 1997 on their Scottish Service. Mr. Howe was evasive when it came to having knowledge of the Afrocentric theorists who were making theoretical arguments; he confused statements of fact with development of theory and could not discern between the one and the other. Furthermore, he seemed more eager to discuss tidbits of personal detail rather than engage in a serious discussion on the demise of hegemonic Eurocentrism.

5. In: *The Afrocentric Idea* I followed the lead of Marimba Ani who had argued in a paper that later became an extended book, *Yurugu* (Africa World Press, 1989) that objectivity was a sort of European subjectivity writ large.

## Chapter Two

1. Schlesinger *Disuniting of America* must be seen in the context of the liberal era when certain whites sought to keep the flame of an integrated society alive where blacks would lose blackness and merge into the white culture as guests. They could not accept blacks on the same footing culturally or otherwise with whites. See in particular, Schlesinger, *The Disuniting of America* (New York: Norton, 1992), p. 73.
2. Molefi Kete Asante, "Multiculturalism: An Exchange," *The American Scholar.*
3. Cheikh Anta Diop, *Civilization or Barbarism* (New York: Lawrence Hill).
4. Theophile Obenga, *African Philosophy in the Context of World History* (Princeton: Sungai, 1998).
5. Aristotle, *Physiognomonica, Vol.6:810a:ff.*

## Chapter Three

1. Maulana Karenga, *Introduction to Black Studies* (Los Angeles: University of Sankore Press, 1993), pp 20-21.
2. Count Constantin Volney, *Ruins of Empire or a Survey of the Revolution of Empires* (Paris, 1791).
3. J. Manchip White, *Ancient Egypt.* (New York: Dover, 1990), p. 10.
4. White, *Ancient Egypt,* pp. 17-37.
5. White, *Ancient Egypt,* pp. 43-60.
6. James Breasted, *The Conquest of Civilization* (New York: Harpers and Brothers, 1926), 8
7. Breasted, *The Conquest of Civilization,* pp. 12-29.
8. Charles Seignobos, *The History of Ancient Civilization* (Paris, 1927).
9. Diodorus, 96.
10. Odyssey, 4:220-28, Diodorus, 97.
11. Diodorus, 98.
12. Herodotus, 2:4.
13. Herodotus, 2:50.

14. Lady Lugard, *A Tropical Dependency* (London, 1906), p. 22.

15. "Nature and Man in Ethiopia," *National Geographic Magazine,* Vol LIV, No. 2, August.

16. Aristotle, *Physiognomonica,* 6:812a:13.

17. Omar El Hakim, *Nubian Architecture* (Cairo, 1993):iii.

18. Thomas Babington Macaulay, "Minute on Education," reprinted in William DeBary, ed., *Sources of Indian Tradition,* (New York: Columbia University Press, 1963), Vol. II, p. 44.

19. Macaulay "Minute on Education," a University Press, p. 45.

20. Ibid., 46.

21. J.F. Lauer, *Observations sur les Pyramides* Paris, pp. 1-3.

22. For a fuller discussion see Maulana Karenga, *Selections from the Husia.* Los Angeles: University of Sankore Press, 1989, and Maulana Karenga, *Maat, The Moral Ideal in Ancient Egypt: A Study in Classical African Ethics.* Unpublished dissertation, University of Southern California, 1994.

## CHAPTER FOUR

1. Mary Lefkowitz, *Not Out of Africa* (New York: Basic Books, 1996).

2. Martin Bernal, *Black Athena* (New Brunswick: Rutgers University Press, 1987).

3. George James, *Stolen Legacy* (Trenton: Africa World Press, 1992).

4. Herodotus,*Histories,* II: 50.

5. Mary R. Lefkowitz and Guy MacLean Rogers, eds., *Black Athena Revisited* (Chapel Hill: University of North Carolina Press), 1996. p.1-522.

## CHAPTER FIVE

1. Mary Lefkowitz and Guy M. Rogers, eds., *Black Athena Revisited* (Chapel Hill: University of North Carolina Press, 1996).

2. Frank Snowden, *Blacks in Antiquity* (Cambridge: Harvard University Press).
3. Lefkowitz and Rogers, op. cit., p. 16.
4. Ibid. p. 27.

## CHAPTER SEVEN

1. K. Appiah, "Europe Upside Down: The Fallacies of Afrocentricity," *Sapina Journal* Vol 5, No. 3(January-June, 1993).
2. Molefi Kete Asante, *Kemet, Afrocentricity and Knowledge.* (Trenton: Africa World Press, 1990).
3. Maulana Karenga, *Kwanzaa: A Celebration of Family Community and Culture* (Los Angeles: University of Sankore Press, 1999), pp127-128.
4. The list of Afrocentrists or those who are like them in the world is inexhaustible and covers every continent because just as soon as a person gains self-consciousness, he or she is on the path to throwing off the Eurocentric veil. This appears to be the destiny of the next millennium's people. No amount of anti-African sentiment can prevent the final overthrow of hegemonic Eurocentrism and it must be defeated, as all other forms of human domination must be defeated, because it was a bad idea from the beginning.
5. Clinton Jean, *Behind the Eurocentric Veil* (Amherst: University of Massachusetts Press, 1990). I am happy to have corresponded with Clinton Jean while he was preparing his book and to have communicated with him just prior to his death. On the eve of publishing his book he spoke concretely of the ways that Africans must move forward the Afrocentric project.

## CHAPTER EIGHT

1. Stephen Howe, *Afrocentrism* (Oxford: Oxford University Press, 1998), p. 1. Howe's book has a bad attitude; it is not correctly turned to positive or constructive engagement with the ideas of the Afrocentrists.

He is immediately in the gutter with snide remarks, innuendoes, and false statements. It is not a serious volume.

2. Howe, op. cit., p. 232.
3. Ibid., p. 233.
4. Ibid., p.250
5. Ibid., p. 257.
6. Howe, p. 250.
7. Samir Amin, *Eurocentrism* (New York: Monthly Review, 1988).

## CHAPTER NINE

1. Miriam Maat Ka Re Monges, *Kush, The Jewel of Nubia* (Trenton: Africa World Press, 1997).

## CHAPTER TEN

1. Gerald Early, "Understanding Afrocentrism," *Civilization* (July-August, 1991).

2. See Tony Martin, *The Jewish Onslaught: Despatches from the Wellesley Battleground* (Boston: The Majority Press, 1996), as well as *The Secret Relationship Between the Blacks and the Jews* (Chicago: Nation of Islam, 1988).

# INDEX